COMPLETE GU

SOAP CARVING

COMPLETE GUIDE TO
SOAP CARVING

Tools, Techniques, and Tips

Janet Bolyard

Fox Chapel
PUBLISHING

© 2018 by Janet Bolyard and Fox Chapel Publishing Company, Inc., 903 Square Street, Mount Joy, PA 17552.

Complete Guide to Soap Carving is an original work, first published in 2018 by Fox Chapel Publishing Company, Inc. The patterns contained herein are copyrighted by the author. Readers may make copies of these patterns for personal use. The patterns themselves, however, are not to be duplicated for resale or distribution under any circumstances. Any such copying is a violation of copyright law.

ISBN 978-1-56523-921-0

Library of Congress Cataloging-in-Publication Data

Names: Bolyard, Janet, author.
Title: Complete guide to soap carving / Janet Bolyard.
Description: Mount Joy [Pennsylvania] : Fox Chapel Publishing, [2018]
Identifiers: LCCN 2018017239 | ISBN 9781565239210 (pbk.)
Subjects: LCSH: Soap sculpture--Technique. | Carving (Decorative arts)
Classification: LCC TT916 .B65 2018 | DDC 736/.95--dc23
LC record available at https://lccn.loc.gov/2018017239

To learn more about the other great books from Fox Chapel Publishing, or to find a retailer near you, call toll-free 800-457-9112 or visit us at *www.FoxChapelPublishing.com*.

We are always looking for talented authors. To submit an idea, please send a brief inquiry to acquisitions@foxchapelpublishing.com.

Printed in Singapore
First printing

Because working with soap and other materials inherently includes the risk of injury and damage, this book cannot guarantee that creating the projects in this book is safe for everyone. For this reason, this book is sold without warranties or guarantees of any kind, expressed or implied, and the publisher and the author disclaim any liability for any injuries, losses, or damages caused in any way by the content of this book or the reader's use of the tools needed to complete the projects presented here. The publisher and the author urge all readers to thoroughly review each project and to understand the use of all tools before beginning any project.

Step-by-step photo illustrations: Janet Bolyard

Studio photography by Mike Mihalo: cover, back cover, pages ii–iii, viii, xi, xii, 3, 4, 5, 6, 7, 8–9, 11, 12–13, 14, 15, 17, 18, 19, 20–21, 22, 25, 26, 27, 28, 29, 30, 31, 32, 33, 34–35, 36, 37, 38, 40–41, 43, 48, 50, 55, 58, 64, 67, 73, 75, 78, 85, 87, 88–89, 90, 91, 92, 93, 98, 102, 105, 112, 114, 117, 120, 123, 126, 129, 134, 137

Page 2 restored advertisement image from Boston Public Library via Wikimedia Commons

Page 22 restored advertisement image from Library of Congress via Wikimedia Commons

Page 28 photo of Brenda Putnam from Archives of American Art via Wikimedia Commons

Shutterstock: pages vi–vii towels: mama_mia, page 1 woodcut: Everett Historical, page 35 superglue: David Brimm, page 37 toothbrush: iMoved Studio, page 37 stickpins: ang intaravichian, page 42 antique Ivory ad: Nagel Photography, page 111: oils P Maxwell Photography, page 111 whisk: Uranium, page 111 microwave: Pro3DArtt, page 111 soap cubes: Rattiya Thongdumhyu, page 111 double broiler: Wichian286, page 111 muffin tray: timquo, page 111 bowl: Khumthong, page 111 coloring: LightSecond, page 131 soap flowers: opportunity_2015, page 132 watermelon carving: TaraPatta, page 133 Sukhothai: Naywan

This book is dedicated to some very special people in my life.
To my husband, Jon, thank you for always being there at my beck and
call when I need wood cut, great ideas, or sharper tools.
A special thank you to our two children, Sean and Crystal, who have
given us many blessings and wonderful grandchildren. Thank you to
all of you soap carvers for your ideas, support, love, and patience as
this hobby has grown over the years. An extra special thanks goes out
to my mom and my brother Jerry, who have encouraged me
for years to pursue my dreams. Dad, I know you are looking down
from heaven with a proud smile on your face. I definitely could
not have accomplished any of this without all of you.

My Mission

There is nothing better than getting a gift that someone handcrafted for you. This special item will be part of your life and possibly the lives of generations to come, and since it was handmade with lots of love, its meaning will far surpass that of any gift mass-produced in some faraway factory.

My aim with this book is to teach the craft of carving and do my part to help keep the art of carving alive. I hope this book inspires those who have the desire to carve, no matter how old or young they are.

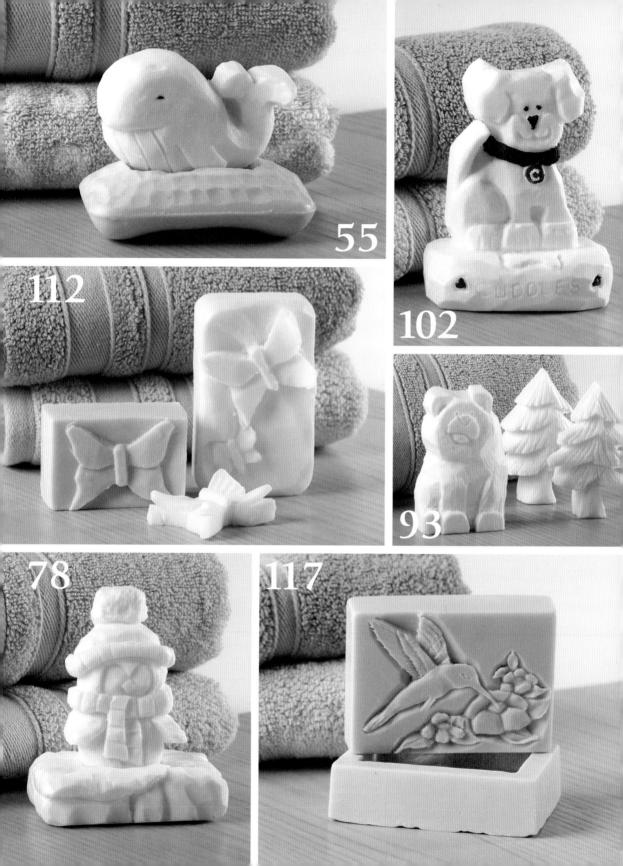

55

102

112

93

78

117

CONTENTS

PART 1: GETTING STARTED

PART 2: CARVING THE NOVICE PROJECTS

PART 3: CARVING THE ADVANCED PROJECTS

PREFACE:
ONE SOAP CARVER'S JOURNEY

My portrait, in airbrush

Beginning at an early age I had a passion for art. In fifth grade in Arkansas City, Kansas (a few moons ago) we had a traveling art teacher who would teach us various projects each week. I always looked forward to this time, because it always made me very happy and it gave me a chance to express myself. Moreover Ms. Perkins was very inspiring. I began to dream of teaching art someday myself. One day, the project she had for us was to sculpt something from a bar of Ivory soap. My first soap carving was a poodle, because that was our family pet. I was so proud of myself because my soap poodle took first prize in the class. My lifelong passion for carving began that day. I still have that feeling of happiness inside me every time I carve.

My mom liked to draw and pursued it for a while before she handed her books over to me. During the summers, she would sign me up for park and recreation programs that were mostly focused on art. Later on in life I found out that my maternal grandfather had been quite a metal fabricator, working in the roundhouse for Rock Island Railways. So it became clear where my love of art and creating originated. Along with my family background, all of the encouragement I have received from my art teachers and family, both then and now, has brought me to my successes today. I have been very blessed to be mentored and encouraged by many renowned woodcarvers from all over the country.

My love for teaching carving came after my 25-year career managing physicians' offices. My husband's career brought us back to Arizona, where I planned on continuing my career in healthcare until retirement. But . . . an opportunity popped up. I found out there was a Woodcraft store near me, so I thought it would be a great time to take a break from unpacking boxes and check it out. To make a short story shorter, they just happened to be looking for a sales representative/woodcarving instructor. I was super excited! I asked my husband, Jon, what he thought of the idea, and you know how

My first project

woodworking tools (especially power tools) make men smile. He'd been dreaming of a new band saw, and my new job could help make that dream come true. My own dream of teaching woodcarving and learning more about woodworking was about to become reality as well. He said yes (of course) and has been very supportive of my woodworking adventure. And yes, he did get his band saw. So I'm proud to say I have been with Woodcraft for ten years now, which has given me the opportunity to teach woodcarving for a living and broaden my knowledge and skills in many aspects of woodworking.

Being an instructor makes me a better carver. To those of you who get the same opportunity, I say seize the day, go for it! There's nothing better than introducing someone new to such a rewarding craft. It always gives me great pleasure to see a student create something entirely on his or her own and then continue growing in confidence and skill to do more challenging projects.

I'm very proud to have written *Complete Guide to Soap Carving*. I hope it inspires you!

Janet Bolyard
www.janetleecarving.com

INTRODUCTION:
WHY CARVE SOAP?

Because it's a lot of FUN! Soap carving gives you an easy way to create sculptures of all sizes using only common bar soap you can get at any store.

For people with a general interest in carving, especially, it's a great point of entry: starting with inexpensive soap and creating your own tools out of upcycled materials is an economical way of finding out if you like carving enough to graduate to knives, gouges, and wood.

Carving soap gives you a way to show your creative side. Who knows, your finished carvings may be good enough to use as centerpieces! If they're really special, your soap sculptures can become family heirlooms. And what's better than handcrafting a personalized gift for someone, for a housewarming or a bridal or baby shower, or any occasion, really!

Soap carving can be practical, too. You can carry through a particular theme of carvings to personalize your bath, kitchen, mudroom, crafts room—wherever soap comes in handy. It's also fun to fancy up your bars of soap with holiday symbols: Halloween with ghosts and vampires, Christmas with Santas and snowmen, and Valentine's Day with hearts, to put a touch of love in the soap dish.

My hope is that you like soap carving as much as I do (which is A LOT, obviously).

WAY BACK WITH SOAP

ca. 2800 BC: Babylonians mix boiling vegetable and animal fats with wood ashes to make the first soap-like substance. They later write their recipes on clay tablets.

ca. 1550 BC: The Ebers Papyrus, one of the world's earliest medical documents, recommends the use of fats plus salts—basic soap—to New Kingdom Egyptians for keeping clean and for remedying skin ailments.

2nd century AD: Philosopher and physician Galen, writing from the Roman Empire, describes a number of different soaps made by different local cultures out of the tallow (fat) of cattle, sheep, or goats, wood ashes, and lye. The high-fat soap made by the German tribes at the time, he wrote, was the best.

SOAP CARVING'S INDUSTRIAL ROOTS

The art of soap carving was born with a marketing campaign. In 1923, Ivory soap manufacturer Procter & Gamble asked public relations pioneer Edward Bernays (1891–1995) to help them fix a problem. The execs told him:

> **"Children hate soap because their mothers wash their faces with soap. The soap gets into their eyes, and they detest it, and obviously if they detest it as children, they'll detest soap when they grow up. What can you do about that?"**
>
> —EDWARD BERNAYS, SPEAKING IN A VIDEO CLIP POSTED BY
> THE MUSEUM OF PUBLIC RELATIONS (*HTTPS://VIMEO.COM/MUSEUMOFPR*)

Bernays's solution: the National Soap Sculpture Competition. And it worked—fantastically. In just a year, more than 20 million kids across the country were carving bars of Procter & Gamble's Ivory brand of soap, even at school. Finalist projects were exhibited in New York City, where they were judged by professional architects and artists. Before long the contest was expanded to allow adults to participate, too.

However, Bernays got the idea of carving soap from someone else. . . Turn to page 28 to find out who it was!

You'll find that besides being a great pastime, soap carving sharpens your detailing skills. And if you keep at it and get involved in the carving community, you'll meet a lot of great people along the way—I know I did!

All of the skills and techniques you learn from soap carving are ones you can take with you when you move on to other carving media—wood, stone, or even fruits and vegetables. Here's an example: I've started a family tradition where I carve faces on carrots for our family barbecues; when the carrots are grilled, they shrivel up and look like old wood spirits. We get a kick out of watching them change. They taste good, too! Whichever direction you take your carving, it makes for great memories and heirlooms, and brings friends and family together even amid busy schedules.

Kids Love It

Ten years ago when I lived in northern California, I was blessed to be part of the Tri-Valley Wood Carving Club. They had a soap carving program to teach kids how to carve. We couldn't make soap carving kits fast enough; at every event the club's soap carving tables were crowded with both kids and adults. Such fond memories! When my husband and I moved back to Arizona and I joined both the Arizona Woodcarvers Association and the Grand Canyon Woodcarving Club, I brought the idea for the youth soap carving program with me. I love seeing kids' imaginations come alive when they create their first projects out of soap, just like mine did, back in school.

Carving bars of soap with wooden tools made from Popsicle or ice cream bar sticks gives kids a safe alternative to knives and wood. It's a good activity, too. For instance, carving a name train for a bedroom or bathroom is a great way to learn how to use tools at the same time as practicing the ABCs! And making soap boats that float in the bathtub is a great way to entertain kids and make bath time more fun at the same time.

As soap carving becomes more and more popular, I would like to challenge carving clubs to initiate their own soap carving programs for kids of all ages. Having a soap carving category during a club's annual competition gives young carvers of all levels a chance to show off their work.

Let It Snow, Let It Snow

Bath Time for Cuddles

A Touch of Summer

Happy Seals

Roses Are Red

There Once Was a Bear

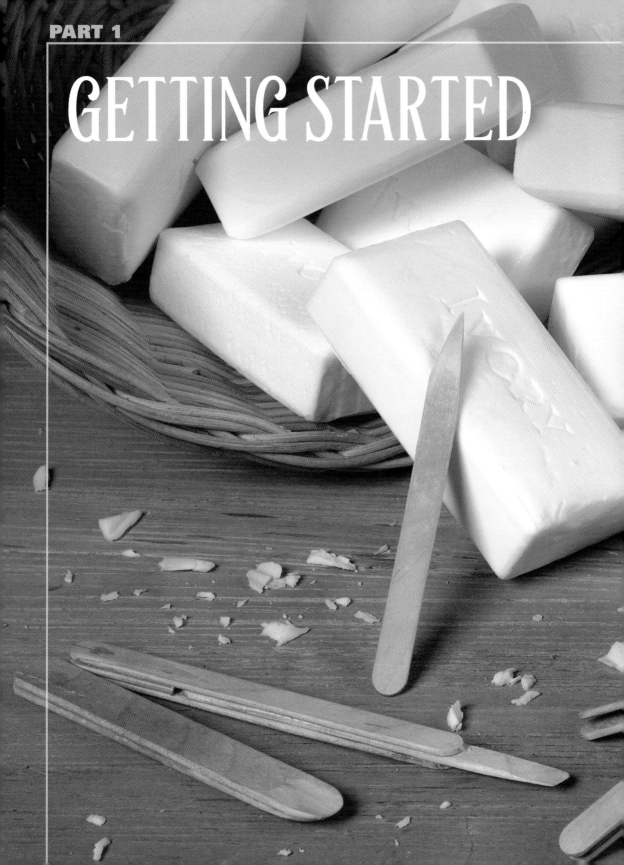

PART 1

GETTING STARTED

MY ADVICE TO BEGINNERS

Keep It Simple

If you're just starting out as a carver, keep your projects simple. Start rough and save the detailing for the end. This way you learn and develop your carving techniques without being overwhelmed by the complexities of doing fine detail work.

Be Sharp About Your Tools

The biggest secret to my success is choosing the appropriate tools for each project and keeping my tools sharp. This book deals extensively with tools and the best ways to make them, handle them, and keep them ready for your next project.

Use the "Stepping Stones"

As an artist, no matter what media you decide to work with, you will experience a few challenges, but please don't be discouraged. I have lived this kind of moment many times, but I've learned to continue until I'm finished. When you get frustrated, step back a few minutes, an hour, or a day—however long you need to reevaluate—and then start carving again. I call this my "stepping stones to carving success," and I've used this method many a time, especially when fatigue sets in.

Adopt the "Pattern Change" Point of View

If you make a mistake, hey, it's okay! Look at it as an opportunity to make "a pattern change." I've had a lot of those, and I've found it has made me a better carver to fix my mistakes—aka make "a pattern change"—than to give up. Most of these pattern changes have ended up happy accidents. So hang in there and keep on carving! Eventually, as your skills develop, people will start to recognize your unique style.

ABOUT SAFETY

Always use your best judgment when working with carving tools. Carving tools are not toys and should only be used for carving.

- Prepare a space with adequate room to carve.
- A carving mat or shelf liner prevents slippage, protects your table surface, and keeps your table clean.
- To keep your clothes soap free, you can choose to wear an apron.

- Wear proper safety glasses to prevent flakes or chips of soap from getting in your eyes. Glasses will also prevent you from accidently rubbing your eyes with soapy hands. If you do get soap in your eyes, ask for assistance from someone near you to help flush your eyes out

LET THE TOOL HIT THE FLOOR

Never try to catch your carving tool when it falls off of your carving table. The odds are high you'll catch the wrong end of the tool. Just let the tool go—sharpening a tool edge is less painful then getting a cut.

GO FRAGRANCE FREE

Some carvers get allergic responses from some soaps. The various fragrances and compounds in the soaps' formulas can affect those who are sensitive to certain scents. I am one of those lucky carvers affected by such reactions. So what I do before getting started is set up a little **desktop fan** and position it so that it draws the fragrance of the soap away from me. This helps me considerably and lets me enjoy my craft.

with water. It may take up to 15 minutes to clear. If symptoms fail to clear, seek medical attention.

- Carve only when you can focus on your work. Don't carve when you are on medication or groggy or tired.
- You'll get the best tool control by having your elbows on the table.
- When possible, carve away from your body, not toward it.
- Keep hands and fingers behind the cutting edge at all times. The hand that is holding the soap needs to be behind the tool.
- For better control, make small, slicing strokes instead of big, hacking ones. Applying too much pressure can cause soap fractures and unwanted soap loss.
- Always clean up after soap carving. A few soap shavings combined with even just a little bit of water can make a floor pretty slippery!
- Keep your carving tools clean and sharp.

HOW TO MAKE YOUR OWN CARVING TOOLS

For many of my projects, I use wooden tools that I've made myself. In my experience, wooden tools are easier to handle and control when carving bars of Ivory soap—they're more effective when smoothing, detailing, and making gentle cuts.

In addition, wooden tools are safer and more economical than metal ones. They can be made quickly and inexpensively to suit your needs for particular carving projects. Wooden knives, gouges, and chisels can be made out of thin, flat, scrap hardwood sticks like wooden dowels, tongue depressors, and Popsicle sticks.

This section of the book will guide you step by step in making your very own wooden soap carving tools.

NOTE: The following direction is deliciously difficult, but someone has to do it . . .

So you need to buy some ice cream or Popsicle sticks, eat the sweet treats, and save the sticks for your future soap carving tools.

Or . . .

You can go to your local craft store and purchase sticks (less fun, but effective).

It's easy to make special shapes with these sticks. You can also create a few specialty tools, such as very narrow or very wide skews and/or chisels. The narrow chisel/skew can be used to carve in tight areas, between the legs of animals, for example, or to clean inside corners or plane a surface smooth. A round-edged scraper works great for fine detailing, cleaning, and smoothing, and for

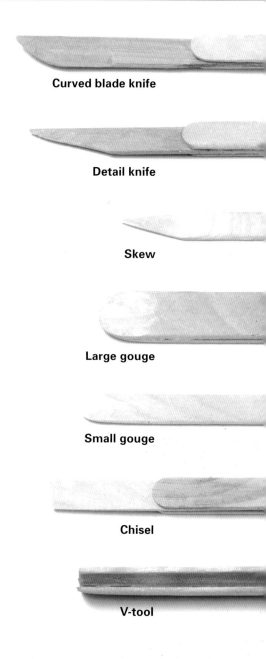

Curved blade knife

Detail knife

Skew

Large gouge

Small gouge

Chisel

V-tool

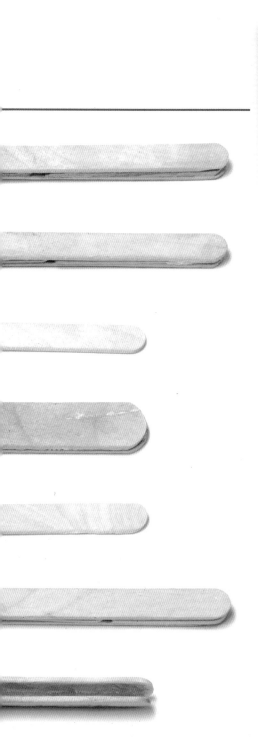

Use a cup of warm water to help keep your tools clean.

outlining or scoring when your project needs more detail or texture. I use a small Popsicle stick.

Alrighty then, let's make some tools!

WHAT YOU'LL NEED

- Popsicles or ice cream bar sticks
- sandpaper in 150 and 220 grits
- coping saw or hobby knife
- paper towels
- wax paper (for drying tools)
- wood glue

- glue brush or extra Popsicle/ice cream stick for glue-ups
- clothespins
- pencil or dowel rod
- triangular/engineer's ruler (for optional V-tool)
- superglue (aka cyanoacrylate, or CA, glue)

MAKE: CURVED BLADE KNIFE

With this knife you can make stop cuts, rough out, and carve fine details—the bulk of your carving work (although I mostly use the similar-but-pointier detail knife).

1. **Mark out the curve of the blade.** Use a pencil to shade out the area to be cut away.

2. **Shape the blade and finish.** By shaping and sanding the cutting edge into a gentle curve, you will need to curve the blade upward. Sand both sides of the blade edge at 20 degrees to get an effective cutting angle.

MAKE: DETAIL KNIFE

As its name suggests, the detail knife works great for carving small details. Its versatility means that it will likely become **your go-to carving tool**.

The detail knife is created the **same way as the curved blade knife** but has a more pointed tip. This tip can be very short to very long.

MAKE: SKEW KNIFE

A skew knife has a straight blade cut at an angle across part of the parallel length of the blade. This is considered a double bevel skew tool since both sides have a tapered bevel. Usually the angle of the bevel on a skew tool should be 20 degrees.

1. Mark out the angle of the blade. Draw a line from the side of the Popsicle tip to one corner of its rounded tip.

2. Shape the blade. Using a hobby knife or coping saw, cut the end of the Popsicle stick at the angle marked out. Repeat on the other side until you get an even blade edge.

3. Sharpen the cutting edge. Hold the cut end of the stick at a right angle to a piece of 150-grit sandpaper and sand, so that the blade edge is straight. The skew knife should come to a sharp point.

4. Finish. To further sharpen the edge, sand the cutting edge with 220- or finer grit sandpaper for a very smooth cutting surface. The skew blade edge is now ready for a handle.

MAKE: EXTENDED KNIFE HANDLE

Although making handles for your wooden soap carving tools is optional, a long handle allows you to carve hard-to-reach areas and a smaller handle gives you more control over finer cuts or gouges. The decision to make a handle should be based on your personal preferences and the demands of your project.

If you prefer a thicker handle, add two sticks to each side of the blade instead of one.

Just make sure it fits comfortably in your hand, and is neither too long nor too short.

Any of the tools in this chapter can be extended with a handle using these instructions.

Place one Popsicle stick on each side of the blade that you've already made. These sticks will become the knife handle. You will need a third stick, cut in half. This short piece will serve as the extension of the blade.

1. Glue the first half of the handle. Apply yellow or white wood glue on one of the sticks that will become part of the handle. Spread the glue evenly and place the blade on top of the glued stick so that 1½" to 2" (4–5 cm) of the handle (stick with glue) is still free.

2. Extend the blade. Glue a short stick onto the free portion of handle with the exposed glue, so that it extends the blade the whole length of the handle. Place glue on the second part of the handle and smooth out the glue. Attach it to the blade on the side where the short stick is visible.

3. Bond the handle and finish. Clamp the glued parts together with a pair of clothespins. Set the knife aside on a piece of wax paper until the glue is dry, about 24 hours to be safe. Then, using a coping saw, cut the handle to the desired length. Round off the corners with sandpaper and the knife is ready for carving.

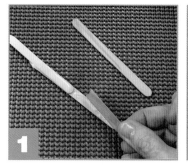

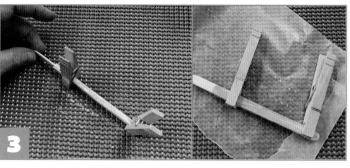

TIP: finish sand your tools' handles with 220-grit or finer sandpaper to rid them of any rough edges for easy handling.

MAKE: GOUGE

A gouge is a square-ended blade that has a concave, trough-like cutting edge. You can make a single- or multilayered gouge. The **sweep,** or curvature, makes **facets** on your medium that lend a textured look—think animal fur, Santa's beard, ocean waves.

1. Make the body of the gouge. Apply yellow or white wood glue on a Popsicle stick and spread the glue evenly on the stick. Place a second stick on top of the first stick. For a deeper gouge, attach a third or even fourth stick. Clamp with a pair of clothespins, wiping off excess glue with a paper towel. Set aside on a piece of wax paper until the glue is dry.

2. Prepare the end. Square off one end of the tool by sanding the gouge body upright over a flat sheet of 150-grit sandpaper.

At this point, your gouge end is flat. There's a bit more sanding ahead . . .

3. Make the sweep. Roll a piece of 150-grit sandpaper around a pencil or a ¼" to ⅜" (0.5–1 cm) wooden dowel rod about the same length as a pencil. Place the rolled sandpaper parallel to the gouge body and sand the square end at an angle. Different sweeps can be achieved by using dowel rods of different widths.

4. Sharpen the blade. Now sand the other side of the sweep until a curved, sharp edge is formed. An effective cutting angle is 20 degrees or more for an aggressive cut. The tapered bevel-edged blade will provide a more transitional cut.

5. Finish. To further sharpen the edge and create a smooth cutting surface, sand the cutting edge and adjacent surfaces with 220- or finer grit sandpaper, as with the other carving tools.

MAKE: CHISEL

Use a chisel's flat, sharp edge to chip carve, plane or smooth soap, or make stop cuts.

1. Flatten the end. Sand the end of the Popsicle stick until it is square at the end.

2. Form a sharp edge. Sand the square edge at an angle (about 20 degrees) on one surface to form a beveled edge.

MAKE: V-TOOL

You don't necessarily need to make a V-tool, since you can make V-cuts with a detail knife (see page 33). However, a V-tool is versatile and fun to use and makes a nice addition to your collection.

If possible, get your hands on a triangular ruler to help shape the V.

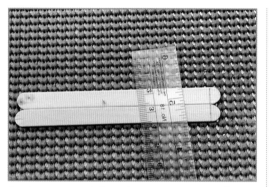

1. Measure sticks. Line up two Popsicle sticks side by side and mark a straight line continuing across the tops of both.

2. Square off the ends. Using a coping saw or hobby knife and sandpaper, square off the ends of the two Popsicle sticks.

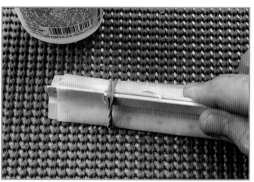

3. Glue the sticks together in a V. Wrap wax paper around the triangular ruler so it doesn't get messy with glue. Set a Popsicle stick on each side and hold tight against ruler. Apply superglue (or CA glue) to where the sticks come together at one end, then the middle. Then apply glue to other end. Let dry on wax paper for 24 hours, and it's ready.

MAKE:
SHARPENING STONES

When your tools are sharp and in good working order, your carving goes so much better, so I'm going to show you how to put together the ultimate DIY sharpening setup.

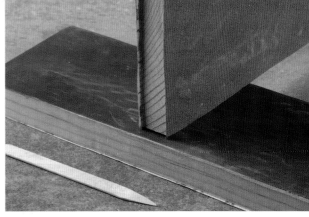

WHAT YOU'LL NEED

- one strip each of 150-, 220-, 320-, and 600-grit sandpaper, each measuring 2" wide x 6"–8" long (5 x 15–20 cm)
- two pieces of wood or MDF (medium-density fiberboard), ¾" or 1" thick x 2" wide x 6"–8" long (2 or 2.5 x 5 x 15–20 cm)

With your four strips of sandpaper and two pieces of wood, you can see that we're going to adhere a different grit of sandpaper to each side of the two wood blocks. One block will have 150 grit on one side and 220 grit on the other; the other block will have the 320 and 600 grits. (This arrangement is totally optional: you can make your own configuration based on your own preferences.) I like to go through all four grits to get an optimal cutting edge on my tools.

1. Prep the wood surfaces. Sand your wood blocks with a separate piece of 150-grit sandpaper to rough up the wood a bit so that the glue will bond well with the sandpaper and wood.

2. Pour on the glue. Apply a couple rows of glue onto one side of the first wood block. Use a glue brush or Popsicle stick to spread the glue evenly across the wood surface.

3. Lay down the sandpaper. Place your first strip of sandpaper, measuring the same length and width as your wood block, onto the wood block. Repeat these steps three times for the other grits.

4. Finish. Set both sharpening stones on wax paper to dry. Once they have dried, you can now clean the soap off your wooden tools while keeping their edges sharp.

ABOUT SOAP

Before I purchase new soap I always give it the "freshness squeeze," by gently pressing in one corner of the soap. If the corner of the bar is hard as a rock, I know the soap is too dry. Carving hard, dry soap tends to be more difficult because it's brittle and chalky. Soft soap is more pliable, making carving much easier. So remember, before beginning every project, always give your soap the freshness squeeze.

Storing Soap

To keep my soap from drying out and becoming hard, I store it in a lidded plastic container or a zip-type plastic bag.

"IT FLOATS" ... BY DESIGN

From 1891 on, the slogan for Ivory famously included the phrase "It Floats." Popular mythology long attributed the discovery of floating soap to an accident in the P&G factory, in which a mixer was left running for too long, but in the 2000s a company archivist discovered that that hadn't actually been the case . . .

James N. Gamble (1836–1932), trained chemist and son of company cofounder James Gamble (1803–1891), had been experimenting with soap formulas that intentionally added more air to his soap formula to make soap that floated. Customers loved it—the floating bar came in handy when doing dishes in a large tub, for instance.

HOW TO MAKE PATTERN TEMPLATES

Most soap carving projects start with a template. You can use the ones from this book, or you can make your own. Or both!

Draw Your Own

If you design your own, keep it simple. No matter what I'm working on, I always keep my drawings basic because even a plain pattern can turn into a complex carving.

I sketch my designs on graph paper with pencil. Graph paper lines help me center my sketches and achieve balance. I measure out rectangle borders equal to the size of the bar of soap I plan to carve. I draw the rectangles in ink so that when I am sketching in pencil, I can erase and make corrections without losing my border.

Copy: Low Detail

If you don't need a lot of details from the pattern, you can make a cardstock template. See pages 138–146 for the templates I carve in this book. You'll also find extra templates that pair well with the projects from the tutorials.

WHAT YOU'LL NEED

- sharp knife
- cutting board
- glue stick
- cardstock (index cards, old holiday cards, or lightweight cardboard)
- pattern template
- measuring tools (I have found having a straight caliper, ruler with depth gauge, and a clear plastic 6-inch ruler are very helpful.)

1. Copy and cut. You could cut the template right from the back of the book, but my advice is to photocopy it instead, so you still have the original design in case you want to carve the same design again later.

2. Glue your pattern onto cardstock. Let dry.

3. Cut out. Use a detail knife to cut out the design.

4. You're done! The next step is to transfer the template to your bar of soap (see page 26).

Copy: High Detail

For pattern templates that have more detail, use **tracing paper**. The procedure for transferring a high detail pattern is different from that of a basic outline; see page 26.

PREP YOUR WORKSPACE AND SOAP

With your tools made and sharpened and your soap bar and template in hand, it's time to get ready to begin carving.

Prep Your Workspace

What I do before getting started is set up a little desktop fan and position it so that it draws the fragrance of the soap away from me. This helps me considerably and lets me enjoy my craft.

Be sure you have good lighting. Good lighting is very important for highly detailed projects.

You'll also need a cup or bowl of hot water near to keep your knife clean and hot.

Save your soap shavings in a baggie or airtight container—they may come in handy later if you need to correct a mistake (see page 35).

Always Start with a Blank Slate

Before carving any bar of soap, it's a good idea to scrape the sides, removing any brand logos or type. Just like a woodcarver sanding her wood before carving, this step is an important one. Besides the logos, it helps get rid of any blemishes or scratches on the soap surface, makes it easier to transfer your pattern, and gives you a fresh canvas to work on.

Use the backside of your knife to scrape your soap bar. The back of your knife should be very straight, allowing you to scrape or plane the surface. I usually scrape all four sides so my soap is nice and smooth and ready to go for carving.

Now you try it: practice by scraping the label off a bar of soap.

HOW TO TRANSFER TEMPLATES TO SOAP BARS

Low Detail Template

WHAT YOU'LL NEED

- toothpick, marker, or detail knife (your marking tool of choice)

Place your template on the bar of soap, centering it so you have plenty of room on all sides to carve. Holding the pattern down, use a toothpick, marker, or detail knife—**your marking tool of choice**—to outline the template on the soap. A marker makes it easier to see the design but it also makes bold lines that can make it harder to see detail on your pattern, so I usually opt for the toothpick. Once you have marked out the complete outline, remove the template from the bar of soap. Mark out additional details with your marking tool of choice (toothpick, marker, or detail knife).

High Detail—"Stickpin Technique"

WHAT YOU'LL NEED

- your tracing paper template
- embroidery pin or stickpin

Center your tracing paper template onto your soap bar. Then use an embroidery pin to poke holes through the tracing paper along all lines of the sketch, both the outline and the interior lines—I call this the "stickpin technique." Before removing the tracing paper, check to make sure all lines have been transferred. You should see a series of pinholes dotting the outline of the pattern when you lift the paper.

I always use a detail knife to make stop cuts over the dots. I usually do not apply a lot of pressure, because I want to prevent bold lines and soap fractures. If a fracture happens, then it's time to fix my mistake. See page 35 if that happens.

ABOUT CARVING

Almost all of the projects in this book fall under two broad categories of carving style: relief carving and in the round.

Relief Carving

Relief carving is when a scene or animal or person—whatever your subject—rises off a flat background surface, in this case the soap bar. The resulting carving is more or less two-dimensional, depending on how high the subject comes up from the background. I have found over the years that high relief carving is my favorite. The reason is because I want my viewer's eyes to stop to really see the whole carving. I find it complimentary when someone takes extra time to look at my work.

Low relief: subject raised slightly from background

Medium relief: greater depth, levels more apparent, shallow three-dimensional effect

In the Round Carving

This style is sculpting in 360 degrees. All surfaces of the subject are carved—there is no background—with the exception of the bottom when the carving stands on a base.

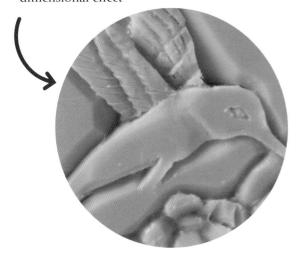

High or "deep relief": deep cuts, pronounced three-dimensional effects, dramatic shadows

Other Kinds of Carving

Caricature style lets you exaggerate features on animals or people, taking an ordinary subject and making its expression or some aspect of it cartoonish. I always set the goal for myself while carving a caricature figurine of evoking a smile or even a chuckle from the viewer.

Chip carving is easy to learn once you have learned to carve reliefs, I have found. You primarily hold the knife the same way and at the same angles: 45 or 65 degrees. I usually hold my knife at a 65-degree angle so I can get great depth and dimension with the soap.

Stylized carving is when depth and detail work are not emphasized in the project.

THE FIRST SOAP CARVER?

Edward Bernays didn't come up with the idea of carving soap out of thin air. Brenda Putnam (1890–1975), a well-known sculptor whose works still stand in the Folger Shakespeare Library and U.S. Capitol in Washington, D.C., first thought of it (in the West, anyway).

In the early 1920s, Putnam wanted an alternative to wax and clay so she wrote to Procter & Gamble about making sculptures out of large hunks of soap—right when Bernays was brainstorming his Ivory campaign . . .

HOW TO HANDLE CARVING TOOLS

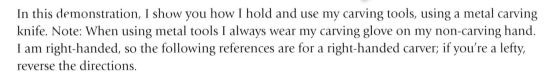

In this demonstration, I show you how I hold and use my carving tools, using a metal carving knife. Note: When using metal tools I always wear my carving glove on my non-carving hand. I am right-handed, so the following references are for a right-handed carver; if you're a lefty, reverse the directions.

Carving Knife (Skew, Curved Blade, or Detail)

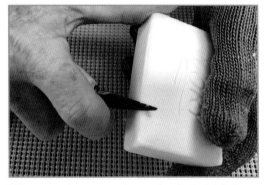

The handle of your knife rests on your pinkie, ring, and middle fingers and upper palm of your hand. Your thumb and your index finger support the tip of your knife. Always remember to have your left hand behind the tool to prevent the tool from cutting your hand.

When carving toward your body (which I generally don't recommend but which I find sometimes necessary), the thumb provides leverage. To prevent a cut from the knife, be sure that the blade travels below the thumb.

ONLY A KNIFE? THAT'S "WHITTLING"!

On occasion the terms "whittling" and "carving" are used interchangeably, but while both involve making shapes out of wood, soap, or other media, really they are two different arts. **Whittling** is using a knife only. You will be amazed what you can do just with a knife. And many of the projects in this book could almost be considered whittling: they are primarily carved with a detail knife.

　　Carving, on the other hand, involves using various types of chisels and gouges in addition to knives.

Push-Thumb Technique

When carving away from your body, the right thumb helps grip the knife. The left thumb provides assistance pushing the blade. This is called the "**push-thumb technique**." You will find you have a lot of control and power behind your knife using this technique.

Palm Tools

The carving tools you've by now made, especially those to which you didn't extend the handles, can be considered "**palm tools.**" Palm tools, as you might guess, fit in the palm of your hand. The index finger and thumb hold the shaft of the tool, while the remaining fingers grip the wooden handle. Choke up on the tool for maximum tool control.

Over the Top

Another way to hold your tool is by using the **over-the-top method** instead of holding the tool like a pencil. With this method, which you sometimes see illustrators or sketchbook artists use, you have better cutting control with your tool and you will experience less fatigue in your hand. You make a cut by gripping and pushing the handle with the help of your other hand.

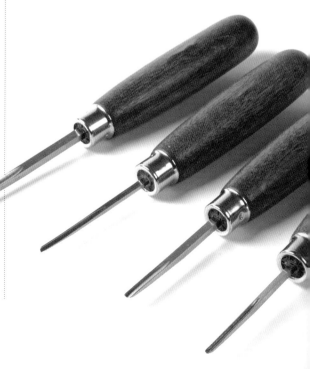

YOUR FIRST CUT: THE STOP CUT

A **stop cut** is used in every style and medium of carving; it's a fundamental technique of the art form. Basically, it's a cut that is used to create a line that will "stop" a knife or other carving tool from going any farther than you want it to. It also helps you establish different layers on your project. You can make a stop cut with a knife, gouge, or V-tool.

There's a reason why the stop cut is so essential to carving: if you don't use stop cuts, you will get a lot of "**tear out**," or a lot of crumbling or missing soap pieces that you'll wish you had to finish your project.

To make a stop cut, draw your knife or gouge along the line of your pattern, pressing down to the depth or level you want to carve to. Be sure you keep your tool vertical, i.e. make this shape: | and not this shape: \ or this shape: /. If your stop cut looks like the latter (\ or /), the overhanging part of the surface of your soap will be very fragile since it has no foundation to support it. When working with soap you won't need to apply much pressure, since soap is a lot more delicate than wood. It's OK to make several strokes to reach the depth you want.

When making a stop cut with a gouge, my go-to gouge is usually a sweep #3 or #4.

I've found that when I'm carving a very tiny or a delicate area where there's a high probability of breakage, I shift gears: First I slow down, and then I start applying less pressure on my workpiece. I make my cuts very shallow and gently carve to the stop cut to clear away unwanted soap to develop a layer or level. (I do the same with wood.) When I carve a rose stem, which is very thin and delicate, I just shave little bit at a time to develop it. Areas that break off easily, I save for last. Sure enough, if I carve them in they will break off; then I might have to start over.

YOUR NEXT CUTS: ROUGHING OUT

Roughing out means to remove large amounts of soap all at once with a knife, gouge, or chisel, thus "roughing out" the shape of your project. It also helps define the levels and elements in the pattern.

Once your stop cut has been made, hold your knife with the tip of your knife going to the stop cut. Run the tip of your knife along the stop cut. Depending on how deep a cut you want, how much soap you have to work with, and how pronounced you want your levels to be, hold your knife at an angle of 45 degrees or 65 degrees.

These first two cuts will release a small V-shaped sliver piece of soap. You are creating an outline that separates different parts of your design. This will also start developing different levels or layers.

When using a gouge or chisel, carve away background soap by pushing your tool into the stop cut so that the soap chips away rather than slices away as when using a knife.

A stop cut can be re-cut many times, so you can slowly develop the depth you want. This technique will create crisp divisions along the patterns lines of your project.

The step after roughing out is **rounding over**.

V-CUT: NO V-TOOL, NO PROBLEM

While a V-tool takes a step or two out of the process and speeds up your carving, you don't really need one. However, there will come a time when you will need to make a V-cut. If you don't have the special tool ready, here's how you do it. First, make a stop cut (see page 31) . . .

1. **Cut one side of the V.** Hold the knife at a 45- to 65-degree angle. Run the knife at an angle along toward the stop cut.

2. **Finish the V-cut.** Turn your piece around and repeat the previous step to finish the V-cut.

ROUNDING OVER

Rounding over means to smooth out rough edges after roughing out your project, usually using a gouge. Turn the gouge over and, gently going away from or toward your body, scrape the edge away. This technique can also be used to carve round objects, like grapes.

TIP: I always have a bar of soap handy to practice a technique on when needed.

HOW TO USE A GO-BY

After roughing out your project, start working on the levels. I have my sketch nearby so I have my pattern "go-by" or blueprint. This helps me keep track of which side of the stop cut I should carve on.

Take a look at the snowman example. Areas that show shadow are deeper than areas that don't show shadow. This is how you differentiate between levels, which helps you develop depth.

Deeper (lower)

Shallower (higher)

HOW TO FIX MISTAKES

No matter the media, you are going to meet some challenges; the majority of the time they are fixable. It's no different with soap. Accidental breaks will happen from time to time. Fortunately, there is more than one way to fuse two pieces of soap together.

Most soap breaks can be repaired by applying a **soap slurry meld** (see below) on the surface of the broken end, then carefully reattaching the broken piece to the body of your project. Once the glue is dry you can carve again.

When You've Carved Off Too Much . . .

You also can be proactive with the slurry meld method. If you have carved away more soap than you should have, restore the area with slurry as needed. Once it's dried, you're back in business!

THE STRONG ALTERNATIVE: SUPERGLUE OR CRAFT GLUE

Superglue (cyanoacrylate, or CA glue) works fine when you're gluing a completed carving to its base. It dries and hardens very quickly to a hard, brittle consistency. But with time it turns a brownish color. Superglue can become difficult to carve through, which can cause you to slip and damage the softer soap areas of your project. Craft glue, meanwhile, sometimes dries to a rubbery, whitish consistency.

If a major glue-up is involved I allow the glue to dry for up to 24 hours.

THE SOAP SLURRY MELD METHOD

Scrape the surface of a bar of soap with your carving knife onto a plate with a little bit of water. Mix the shavings and water together to form a thick soap slurry. Use the slurry to stick the broken piece back to the bar, under pressure.

After application and drying, the soap slurry welds the soap together as it is essentially all the same material.

You also use this method to weld two soaps together (as in the soap-on-a-rope projects)—see page 71.

TIP: Do not use any other glue if you wish to detail the carving further.

HOW TO ADD DETAIL AND TEXTURE

Scales, feathers, fur, clumpy snow, eyes, noses—after you have finished carving the shapes of your project, it's time to really bring it to life with fine details and texturing. Detailing defines smaller, more intricate areas. For most detail work I use small V and U (veiner) gouges or a detail knife, but for special features I switch to specialty tools.

For the Snowman and other projects, I slathered on soap chips to add texturing effects.

For beards, use a V-tool to draw elongated S curves.

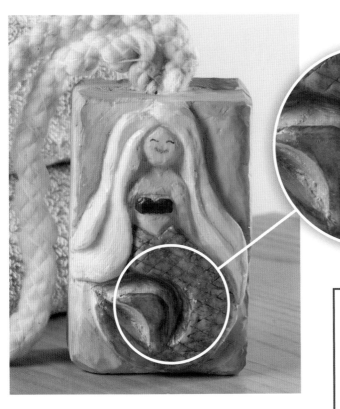

Crisscross cuts simulate scales.

> **TIP:** I always keep an extra bar of soap nearby to practice a cut or try out a new technique. For instance, before carving the Soap-on-a-Rope Mermaid project, I practiced making scales before adding them the mermaid's tail.

HANDY DETAILING AND TEXTURING TOOLS

Fur Texturizer. Use a medium toothbrush to create an interesting texture that resembles animal fur.

Eye and Nose Detailer. An embroidery pin, stickpin, or sewing needle that doesn't bend easily is helpful when outlining and detailing eyes and noses. It also can bore small holes for eyes, noses, or even starfish skin.

ABOUT FINISHING

To give your soap carvings a smooth veneer you need to sand and smooth out rough edges. Then you can decide whether to decorate with paint, preserve the soap's natural color with a lacquer seal, or leave the soap carving raw so it can be used as soap. Regardless of what you make your projects for, I strongly encourage you to avoid over-painting—you don't want to take away too much of the unique textural qualities of soap.

WHAT YOU'LL NEED

- two paintbrushes (or any small disposable brushes) for cleaning the soap debris from your carving—kind of like when archeologists dust off their bony finds
- sponge (optional)
- paintbrushes for painting (optional)
- lacquer
- warm water
- lidded plastic container or zip-type plastic bag

TOOLS FOR TIDYING WHILE YOU CARVE

Chip Remover. I picked up a great tip from a seasoned carver many years ago: Buy a ¼" (0.5 cm) wooden dowel rod. Cut it to the length of a pencil. Sharpen one end to a fine tip with a pencil sharpener. This pointed tool comes in handy for cleaning unwanted chips and slivers of soap out of nooks and crannies in your projects.

Dry Brush. Over the years, I have found that it is helpful to have a soft, dry brush to remove tiny flakes, slivers, and chips of soap as I'm carving. I use a ½" (1 cm) soft art brush.

INTENDED USE	TYPE OF FINISH	WHAT'S NEEDED
in sink or tub	raw	no finish
for display or gift	lacquer	1 coat of satin lacquer
for display or gift	painted	1 coat satin lacquer, paint, 2–3 coats satin and/or glossy lacquer

The Wet-Sanding Technique

After I have finished the "carving" part of my soap carving, I dry brush once again, and then I wet sand. The wet-sanding technique is the last step of finessing your project. I use a separate brush for this step—one that is long-haired and flexible (⅛"–¼" [0.31–0.5 cm]). A flexible brush will flow gently across the soap surface and clean hard-to-reach areas. You will be amazed how well a little warm water plus a brush cleans and seals the soap surface. A sponge or even wet Popsicle stick will work in a pinch.

After I have cleaned my carving with this technique, I can see if more carving is needed. Once I'm sure all the carving is done, I smooth out areas again to get rid of any imperfections. It's like sanding soap with water: your soap carving becomes more uniform, with a nice polished look.

Soaps for Display: Seal with Lacquer

First of all, **do not** seal soap carvings that are intended for bath or sink time!

For projects that I want to last or put up for display, even non-painted projects, I apply a lacquer spray as a seal against dirt and loss of moisture.

For projects I decide to paint, before painting I spray a light coat of satin lacquer, which serves as a **primer**, or **undercoat**. This undercoat seals in the soap's moisture and allows my paintbrush to flow smoothly across the soap. It also ensures a better

adhesion of the paint to the soap surface. After painting, I apply a thick **top coat** of lacquer so my project is well sealed and protected from dust and water for years to come.

- For a flashy, glossy look: gloss lacquer (see Soap-on-a-Rope: Pirate, page 73, and Soap-on-a-Rope: Mermaid, page 75)
- For a more natural look: satin lacquer (all other projects)

Brushes for Painting

I usually use inexpensive synthetic brushes—a round (size #4) brush for outlining, filling in small areas, and making thin to thick lines; a detail round (size #1) brush for detailing tiny areas and making short strokes; and a short liner (size #2) brush for long, flowing detail lines or stripes or tight circular motions.

FINISH WITH FLAIR

For some of my more detailed projects, instead of spraying one kind of lacquer over all the soap's surface, I use a brush and apply different lacquer sheens on different areas. So, for instance, I might brush-lacquer the pirate's pants with a satin, his shirt a semi-gloss, and his boots a full gloss. This way, the light reflects differently from different parts of the carving, which moves the eye in interesting ways.

CARVING THE
NOVICE PROJECTS

IVORY ALL THE WAY

The projects in Part 2 are carved from Ivory soap bars. I've tried other soap bars and have found them usually chalky, hard, dense, and dry—and challenging to carve. Okay, I confess, I'm partial to Ivory soap, since it was my first carving medium. Still, it has so much to offer (besides sentimental value): it's soft, airy, delicate, easy to work with, and it smells good, too! With these attributes, Ivory is hands down the best soap with which to learn how to carve. Ivory is very reasonably priced, and with the use of handmade tools, which are all Part 2 calls for, there's not a lot invested.

Wooden tools are my tools of choice with Ivory soap. But just because they are wooden does not mean they are any less effective. Ivory's airy texture means that a delicate touch is essential as you carve your first projects. Soft, smooth cuts will give you the results you're looking for.

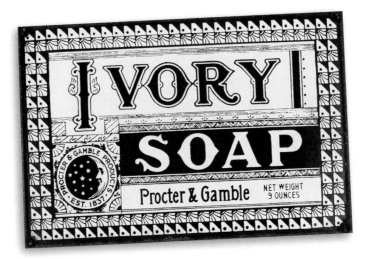

Harley Procter, son of Procter & Gamble cofounder William Procter, got the name for the Ivory soap brand from Psalm 45:8:

*All thy garments smell of myrrh, and aloes, and cassia, out of the **ivory** palaces, whereby they have made thee glad.*

It's important to find a subject matter that you want to carve. You will notice that some of the projects in this book are holiday themed. After all, who doesn't like holidays?

First we carve to celebrate Valentine's Day. A charming little heart in a soap dish, along with a few x's and o's (see Gallery, page 6), will certainly set the holiday mood.

This project is simple but introduces you to two different styles of carving: relief and in the round. You will also learn tool technique, repairs, and working with soap as a medium.

WHAT YOU'LL NEED

- 1 Ivory bar
- marking tool of choice
- carving knife
- large gouge
- 2 brushes, water

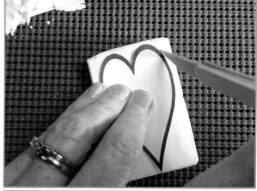

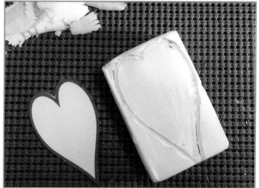

2. Hold the template down while you outline the template pattern. You can use a detail knife, toothpick, or marker. Outline around the template with your marking tool of choice.

1. Using the back of your knife or a straight edge, plane off the logos on both sides of the soap bar. Then set the template in the center of the bar.

3. Make a stop cut. Remember to keep your knife vertical and going downward.

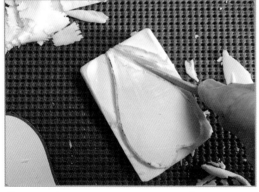

5. Use a large gouge, holding it upside down, to round off the edge.

4. Rough out. Holding your knife at a 45-degree angle, cut along the stop cut. If you're getting a lot of chipout, redo the stop cut and gently scrape away any tiny chips. This not only removes the chips, it cleans and smooths the soap at the same time.

6. I use a soft, dry brush to remove small chips. Congrats—you've done a relief carving! Next we'll go "in the round."

7. Make a stop cut, holding the tool vertically and cutting downward until the tool cuts all the way through the soap. Continue working your way around the design until all waste is removed.

9. The sides can have some unevenness. Smooth them down with your knife.

8. Rotate your soap for easy visibility and cutting.

10. If there is significant chipout, make some soap slurry with your shavings and water. Shape and form the heart using the wet sand technique.

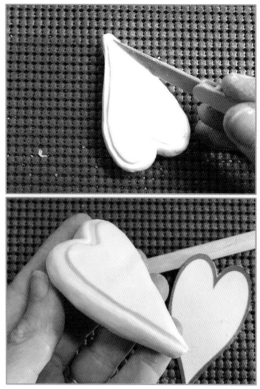

11. Embellish and finish.

EYES WIDE OWL-PEN

30 MIN

You can make this hard-staring owl as simple or as complex as you want—think of the template as only a suggestion. You can give him feathers galore across a chest that looks like a ruffled shirt, a bow tie for a sophisticated look, or you can keep it simple—it's up to you!

WHAT YOU'LL NEED
- 1 Ivory bar
- template and go-by (see page 138)
- detail knife
- stickpin
- large gouge
- small gouge
- 2 brushes, water

1. Prep your soap and center and outline your template. Using tracing paper, transfer details to the soap by using a stickpin to poke holes through the paper.

2. Remove the paper and make stop cuts connecting the dots to make lines.

3. Use a large gouge to smooth and round the edges.

4. If you like, add more detail such as feathers textured across his chest and along his sides. However, you can see that I chose to leave my owl with a more stylized look.

TEDDY BEAR

45 MIN

It doesn't matter how young or old you are, everybody loves teddy bears.

This project can be either very simple or complex depending on the level of detail you add. Notice the number of different levels I carved to give him a three-dimensional look. His ears are the lowest level of his head. He has a fat tummy, so it will be higher than his arms and legs. His nose is the highest level of his face. To keep track of what's above what in your carving, always have your go-by nearby.

WHAT YOU'LL NEED

- 2 Ivory bars
- template and go-by (see page 138)
- detail knife
- toothpick
- ruler
- penny
- large gouge
- small gouge
- 2 brushes, water

The Flat Car

1. Prep your soap. Notice that two separate bars will be needed for this project (unless you reduce the size of the bear template).

2. Outline both patterns onto the two bars of soap—bear on one, train car on the other.

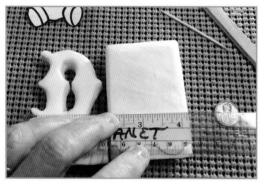

3. I used a previously carved train car as a guide. I lined it up with the new flat car that I was cutting out. I used my clear plastic ruler as a guide. I needed them to match and be the same height.

4. Deepen the stop cut. Now the pattern outline is visible.

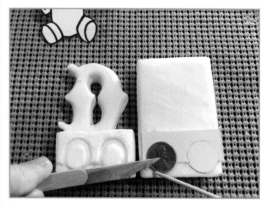

5. I used my penny as the template for the wheels.

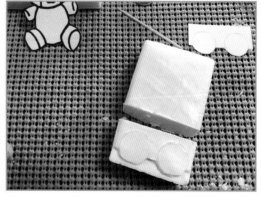

6. Gently, continue to deepen the stop cut until you have completely gone through the soap.

7. Using the gouge, smooth and round the edges of the wheels.

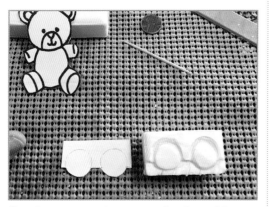

8. Flat car complete! Now for the teddy bear . . .

Teddy Bear

9. Prep your soap as usual. Center the template and mark the outline with a toothpick.

10. If necessary, deepen your markings to see the outline easier. Mark out the details of the face, legs, arms, and feet. I always have my go-by nearby so I know which side of the stop cut to cut on.

11. Start carving under the bear's chin and on top of his head. Notice which side of the stop cut I carved to: because I want the head to stand forward, I carved to the head, both under the chin and from the ears. Next carve toward the body on both the arms and legs. This way his tummy stands forward. You are starting to set up levels and add depth. Leave the base of the bear squared off, so he can sit balanced on the flat car.

12. Deepen your stop cuts on the facial features. Make sure your tools are clean and sharp, especially when working on facial details of any kind. The face is the focal point that everyone first looks at, so it is important that the cuts are clean and clear of chipout. I wanted the nose and muzzle to stand forward. To do this, I carved toward the stop cut. This drops the face and brings the muzzle forward. Outline the nose and mouth a little bit more. Gently remove soap away from the nose and mouth to add more definition.

13. Use the large gouge to round over the edges of the bear's body, arms, and legs.

14. Periodically clean off your project with a dry, soft-bristle brush.

15. Use the small gouge to create concave half-moons for the insides of the ears. At the same time, smooth and round the areas for his feet.

17. The carving is complete! Now you can decide if you want to further personalize the bear or leave him as is.

16. Use the wet-sanding technique to smooth the entire bear.

WHALE OF A TALE

This project is fun to carve, yes, but the real fun happens in the bathtub. Oh, the adventures that the whale's creator will share! Not only is this happy whale fun at bath time, it can also be ready for action near a sink to clean dirty hands. I know this because I have a whale near my own sink, carved by one of my granddaughters.

The whale can be carved into the reverse side of the soap-on-a-rope projects (see pages 73 and 75). Carved in the round, as here, it can be set upright on its own base of Irish Spring ocean waves.

WHAT YOU'LL NEED

- 1 Ivory bar, 1 Irish Spring bar for base (optional)
- template and go-by (see page 138)
- marking tool of choice
- carving knife
- small gouge
- large gouge
- V-tool
- 2 brushes, water

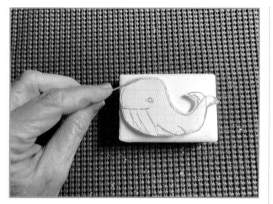

1. Prep the soap. Center your template and outline with your marking tool of choice.

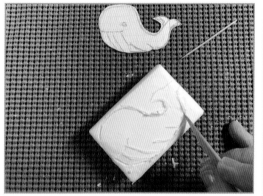

2. Use a detail knife to make stop cuts.

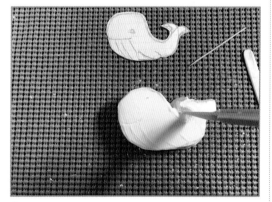

3. Leave extra soap around the tail to decrease the chances of the tail breaking off during carving.

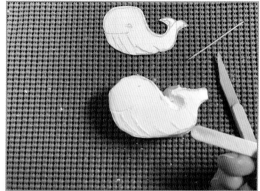

4. Using a small gouge, carve the area between the tail and the body. Then scoop out soap until you can peek through.

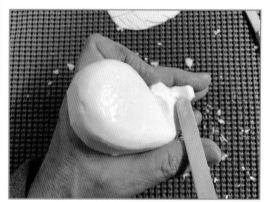

5. I wanted my tail to have movement. Using a small gouge, I added concavity to the end of the tail. This gives the tail more dimension—more natural looking than a flat tail. Note how I'm supporting the backside of the tail while I carve. This prevents the tail from breaking.

6. Use all your tools to smooth and clean every part of the carving before you begin detailing.

7. Using a detail knife, mark out the mouth and the underbelly lines. You can make a V-cut with a detail knife, especially in tight workspaces.

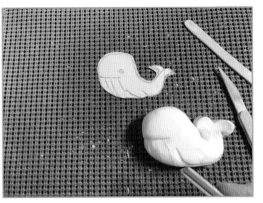

8. Otherwise, use your V-tool where space allows. First make a stop cut, then go back over the cut with the V-tool. Not only does the stop cut serve as a helpful guide, it also helps makes your cut cleaner.

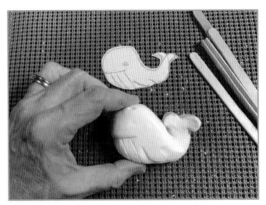

9. Dry brush, wet sand, and detail. Now you have a whale of a tale to tell!

CHUGGA-CHUGGA NAME TRAIN!

2 HRS

Carving a name train is a great way for younger carvers to personalize their bedroom or bathroom and to show off their skills and creativity. Children can learn their letters, practice spelling their names, and get comfortable with soap carving. Older kids and teens can add more advanced details to this project.

WHAT YOU'LL NEED

- 2 Ivory bars plus 1 bar for each letter
- templates and go-bys (see page 139)
- marking tool of choice
- ruler
- penny
- chisel
- large gouge
- small gouge
- 2 brushes, water

Engine

1. We begin with the engine. To get a nice clean slate, we plane off the logos from both sides of the bar.

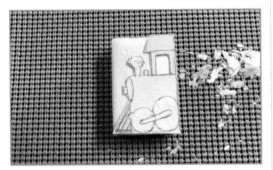

2. Center your template on the bar of soap.

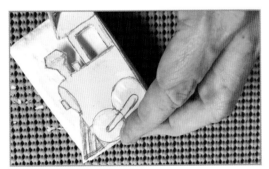

3. Outline the train using your marking tool of choice. Mark in the roofline, headlight, and other lines.

4. Use a ruler and, on your template, measure the distance from the front of the grill to the front of the first wheel. Transfer the measurement to the soap bar.

5. I used a penny as my template for my first wheel and then I marked out the second wheel with the same penny. The coupling rod can wait until near the end of the project along with other finishing details.

6. Rough out. Make a stop cut with the detail knife; then, holding the knife at a 45-degree angle, carve toward the stop cut.

Remove a thin layer of soap at a time since soap can chip or break off easily, especially if it's a little dry. Repeat, taking off layers until all soap is removed, until you have a clean outline.

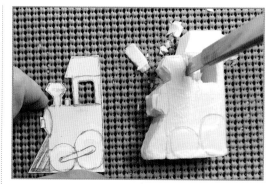

9. Continue roughing out. In delicate areas, apply only light pressure with your chisel.

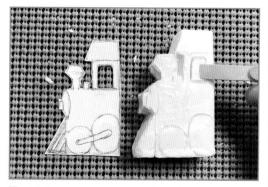

7. Make stop cuts along the window lines with the detail knife or chisel. Chisel out the soap layer by layer. Remake the stop cuts as needed to prevent chipping away too much of the window's straight lines.

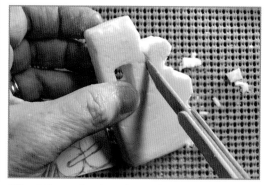

10. When piercing through, it is helpful to approach from the backside of the project. This assures that your cut is straight from front to back.

8. Continue to bore out the soap until you can peek through the window.

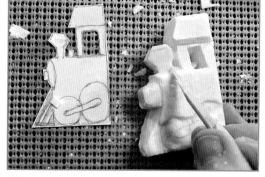

11. Using your detail knife, continue to add details to the engine. Round over the edges of the engine body. Mark out the coupling rod.

12. Use your large gouge to round over the wheels. I usually have my small crockpot with warm water nearby to clean off my tools so I get the cuts I'm expecting. Notice that I have the gouge turned upside down. Not only does this create roundness, it also smooths the soap to a clean edge with no chipouts.

13. Do a little wet sanding to clear away small, uneven areas. Then go back and reestablish detail as needed with your detail knife.

Letters

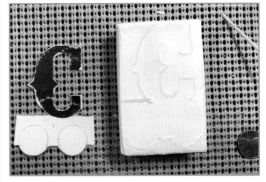

14. Prep your next bar of soap. Center the template of your first letter on the bar and outline the pattern. Each letter stands on its own flat car. Outline the basic shape of the car, then use a penny for the wheels.

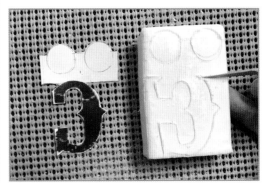

15. I recreate my outlines with a deeper stop cut for a better visual read of my lines. I always have my go-by near me so I can stay on track of what I'm supposed to be carving and what I'm not supposed to be carving. I always rotate my project around so it's easier to carve and I have better control of my tools.

16. Use a small gouge to make the smaller curvatures of the letter C. Make the stop cut with your knife or gouge; then carve toward the stop cut. Go layer by layer until you have gone completely down to the level you want to reach. In this case, you are going completely through the soap.

17. Using your knife, start adding fine details. Round off the edges with your knife. Also use your large gouge turned upside down to round over the edges of the letter and the wheels.

18. Wet sand to smooth out rough edges.

19. I kept the bottom square so the train car would stand up on its own. Etch diagonal lines to look like railroad track. Repeat to make the rest of letters.

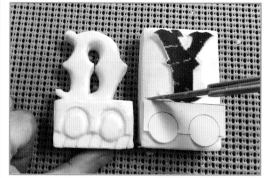

20. When moving from letter to letter, place each new flat car next to the previous car with letter to make sure they are the same height and size.

Caboose

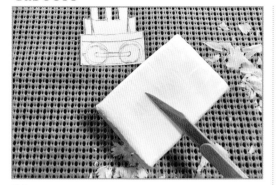

21. Now we work on the caboose. Prep your soap bar then center your template and outline.

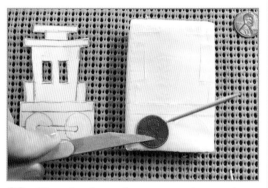

22. The wheels go the same as the previous cars. Rough out the coupling rod.

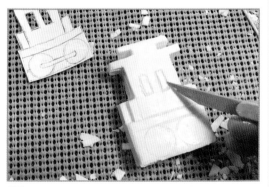

23. Deep stop cuts help me better visualize outlines.

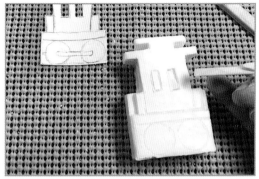

24. Bore out windows with your chisel.

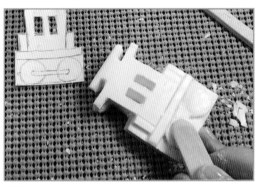

25. Now add the fine details.

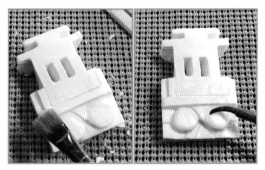

26. Dry brush and wet sand until the project looks and feels complete!

THE "IT FLOATS" SAILBOAT

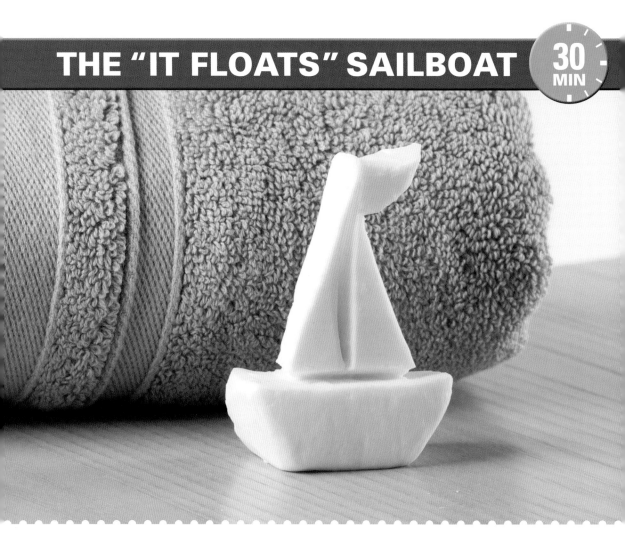

This project is bound to be a hit with boat lovers. In fact, you can carve a fleet of boats of all kinds, shapes, and sizes. And just as the old slogan (see page 22) suggests, boats carved from Ivory soap and given a wide base, or "hull," will float!

WHAT YOU'LL NEED

- 1 Ivory bar
- template and go-by (see page 139)
- marking tool of choice
- ruler or straightedge
- detail knife
- chisel
- 2 brushes, water

1. Center the template on the bar after prepping it for carving, and outline the template.

2. I like to use a clear, flexible, six-inch ruler to check that my lines are straight. With your lines drawn, make deeper stop cuts to outline the design. This makes the design easy to see.

3. Make stop cuts. Then, holding your detail knife at a 45-degree angle, start carving away the bottom sides of the boat. You can also use a chisel or skew knife.

4. Keep working your way around the boat. Leave extra carving space around the flag so it is stable until you are ready to detail it, near the end. Tiny, delicate areas can break off easily if the project is being moved around a lot.

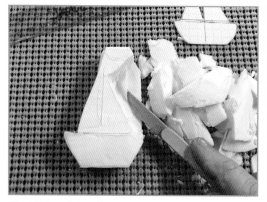

5. Chip, chip, chip away!

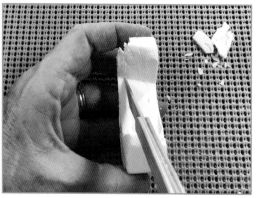

6. Tidy up the sides.

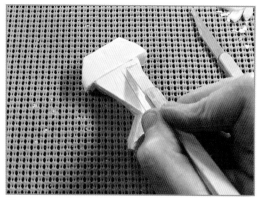

7. Add details with your knife and chisel.

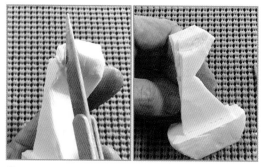

8. I supported the backside of the flag as I gently carved away excess soap. Notice how much extra soap I left around the flag to be carved later.

9. I held the soap steady as I made my final cuts.

10. Wet sand, detail, and finish to your preferences. Ahoy!

Carving all three of these treasures will give you practice in a variety of techniques, including adding detail and texturing. You'll need one Ivory bar per "treasure," as well as the standard tools: something to mark lines, a carving knife, a gouge, and brushes and water. A clay-sculpting tool (see page 92) and V-tool could come in handy, too. See pages 140, 141, and 145 for the templates and go-bys.

45 MIN Seahorse

1. Prep your soap bar and center your template as usual. Then outline with your marking tool of choice. I used a toothpick.

2. Add details with a toothpick, clay-sculpting tool, or detail knife.

3. Use a detail knife to clean crevices under the chin. Now, give this little seahorse some character by detailing his snout and adding lines on his chest and belly.

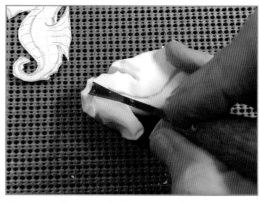

4. A small gouge helps make the scalloped areas of his mane, tail, and fins. What a beauty!

1. Once you've prepped your soap bar and centered the template, you need to transfer the template to the soap. The "stickpin technique" (see page 26) is my preferred method.

2. After outlining with stop cuts, it's time to rough out. Hold your knife at a 65-degree angle and cut toward your stop cut. Work your way all the way down and around the whole project.

3. Make more stop cuts to add texture.

4. Use your V-tool and run a pass over each of the stop cuts you've just made.

5. After making passes with a V-tool, go back over your work with a detail knife to clean and redefine the passes. Dry brush, wet sand, and you're done!

1. Transfer the template to the soap bar and outline.

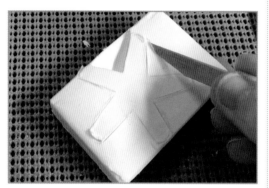

2. Make your stop cut. Then, holding the knife at a 65-degree angle, cut toward the stop cut to rough out.

3. Cut down and around the project until you have carved away all surrounding soap. The starfish should be coming into definition now.

4. Start rounding the edges with a gouge (I used a metal #3). Notice that my tool is upside down.

5. Use a toothpick to add texture.

Soap-on-a-rope always made bath times more fun for my children when they were growing up. It's practical, too: hanging up your soap between uses keeps your soap from turning into a soggy pile of mush.

This tutorial shows you how to make soap-on-a-rope. Then, in the following pages, you learn how to personalize your bars with any number of characters, including a rugged pirate—you can almost hear him say "Aaarrggghhh!"

WHAT YOU'LL NEED

- 2 Ivory bars
- 18" (45 cm) of soft ply rope
- 2 small clamps
- chisel
- soap slurry (see page 35)

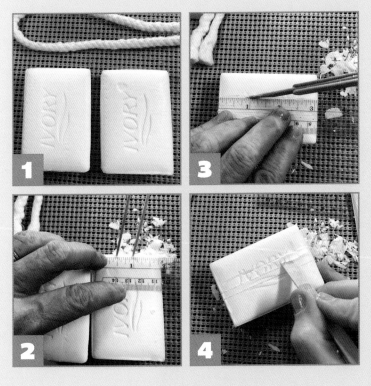

1. This project requires you to soap-glue two bars together. The rope travels through a channel carved in one bar of soap. For the rope, check your local fabric/hobby store.

2. Using a ruler, locate the center of one soap bar. Carve out a ½" (1 cm)-wide channel down the center of the bar. I mark out the channel with toothpicks.

3. Make a stop cut lengthwise for the channel. The channel will be about ½" (1 cm) deep—the depth depends on the thickness of your rope.

4. Use your chisel to bore out the channel.

5. To get clean, straight lines, repeat your stop cuts and then chisel out the extra soap.

6. Chisel out the channel.

7. Make some soap slurry with some of your soap shavings. Small shavings are better than bigger chips. Add enough water to make a thick slurry.

8. Layer the slurry in the channel. Then lay your rope in the channel and cover it with more soap slurry.

9. Slather a generous amount of slurry over the whole bar.

10. Squeeze the two bars together. Add more slurry to fill in gaps.

11. Apply a generous amount of soap slurry around the edges. Once the slurry dries, it can be planed off to a smooth surface.

12. Clamps work better than rubber bands. Rubber bands will cut into soap, leaving unwanted cut lines and marks. Leave the soap bars clamped for 24 hours to cure. Then you're ready to embellish!

SOAP-ON-A-ROPE PIRATE

Arrrggghhh . . . matey! Where be the treasures of gold and jewels? Are they beyond Bubble Mountain Terrain?

This is a great project to be used for decoration or treasure finding fun in the tub.

For extra templates, see page 140.

WHAT YOU'LL NEED

- 1 soap-on-a-rope (see page 71)
- template and go-by (see page 139)
- marking tool of choice
- stickpins
- toothpick
- detail knife
- gouge
- 2 brushes, water

1. Notice that I have two patterns, one on cardstock and the other on tracing paper. When I have very detailed patterns, I use both of these.

2. Center and outline the cardstock template.

3. Outline the pirate pattern with the blue marker. Then place your transfer paper on the soap, lining up the outline over the marker. Then, with a stickpin, go over all the interior lines of the pattern, poking a series of dots in the soap. Follow the lines with a multiple pin pokes. When you remove the transfer paper you will see the series of dots created by the stickpin.

4. With a toothpick, gently connect the dots with a thin line. This will guide the stop cuts.

5. Now make stop cuts with your detail knife, carving along the lines. For fine details like the fingers, thumb, and eye, I prefer a toothpick.

6. Follow your go-by so you know which side of the stop cut to carve on.

7. This is a low- to medium-relief carving. On the backside, you can embellish your project with more pirate-themed ideas—an anchor, skull, with crossbones or . . .

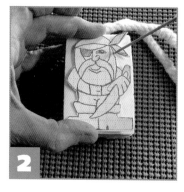

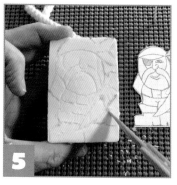

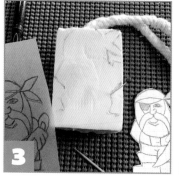

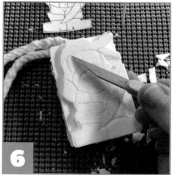

SOAP-ON-A-ROPE MERMAID

Just like the pirate, the mermaid is a blast to make, from start to finish—especially the decorating part! To the backside, add a starfish, shells, or even whales so you can see your handiwork on both sides. If you're really into mermaids, you can carve a whole school of them for different purposes: for practical use, to display on their own, or as part of a themed display.

WHAT YOU'LL NEED

- 1 soap-on-a-rope (see page 71)
- template and go-by (see page 140)
- marking tool of choice
- stickpins
- toothpick
- detail knife
- gouge
- 2 brushes, water
- small gouge (optional for scale texturing)

1. Center the template and outline. I used a marker to make it easier to line up the transfer paper over the outline. Then, with a stickpin, go over all the interior lines of the pattern.

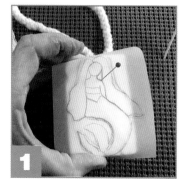

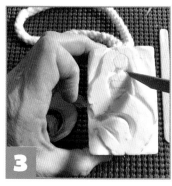

2. When you remove the transfer paper you will see the series of dots made by the stickpin. Now take your toothpick and gently make a thin line to connect the dots. The stop cuts will come easy.

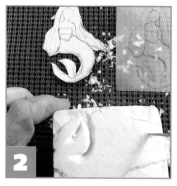

3. Using your detail knife make stop cuts on all lines of the design. Follow your go-by so you know which side of the stop cut to carve on.

4. Use your gouge to round and smooth the edges of her hair and the edges of her face.

5. Wet sand, then do some texturing on her tail. You can make a crisscross pattern or use a small gouge to make fish scales. Just be sure your tool is clean and sharp for crisp lines.

WORKSHOP: MORTISE AND TENON

If you want to create a soap project that stands upright on a soap base, the mortise-and-tenon joint used in traditional woodworking is the best way to keep the two pieces together. A **mortise** is formed by carving a rectangular groove in the large, flat surface of one bar of soap. The small-end dimensions of the second soap bar—the **tenon**—determine the dimensions of the mortise.

WHAT YOU'LL NEED

- 2 soap bars
- water and dish for slurry making (see page 35)
- clamps
- paint
- carving knife
- chisel

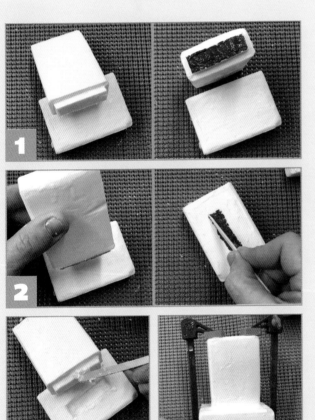

1. Paint it. If you need help with centering the tenon on the base, paint the end of the tenon and it will act as a stamp.

2. Stamp it. Mark the base where you will excavate the mortise. With the outline of the tenon stamped in place to help guide you, now you can bore out the mortise. Remove the traces of paint with a detail knife.

3. Ready for glue-up. Using a glue brush or Popsicle stick (I use the latter), spackle the exposed surfaces of both the mortise and the tenon with melded soap slurry. You can also use glue.

4. Attach base to block. While the glue is still wet, insert the tenon at a right angle in the mortise. By gently squeezing or clamping the mortise and tenon together, and then allowing the joint to dry overnight, you will get a very strong weld between your carving block and its base.

45 MIN

Here's a good project to introduce you to caricature-style carving. I'm fond of doing caricatures since it brings so much personality to my work. This cool bird will look adorable near a bath, sink, shelf, or even on a windowsill.

WHAT YOU'LL NEED

- 2 Ivory bars
- template and go-by (see page 141)
- detail knife
- marking tool of choice
- small gouge
- 2 brushes, water
- chisel

Color gives him even more personality! See page 38 for finishing tips.

1. Prep your soap and center your template. Hold it steady on the soap bar as you outline.

2. Mark out the rough details of the pattern. I will add the eyes, beak, scarf, and stocking cap details near the end of project.

3. Let's start the roughing out process. Make a stop cut along the outer lines of the pattern, applying gentle pressure to prevent chipout. Be sure your stop cuts are completely vertical!

4. Now cut away excess soap.

5. Beginning at the top, make a stop cut on the bottom of the stocking cap tassel.

6. Holding your knife at a 45-degree angle, cut along the bottom of the stop cut. This creates a shadow. The broader the angle, the deeper the shadow will be, and the more dimension the carving will have. Cutting at a 65-degree angle also creates a good amount of depth and dimension.

7. Keep working your way down the project. Make a stop cut, and then a rough-out cut going toward the stop cut (a, b, and c). The second cut is very important because it differentiates the levels. I always have my go-by to help me stay on track with the design. As I carve, I rotate my soap—this gives me better control of my tool cuts (d–i).

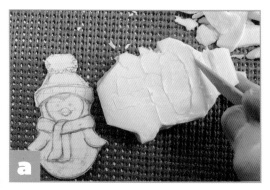

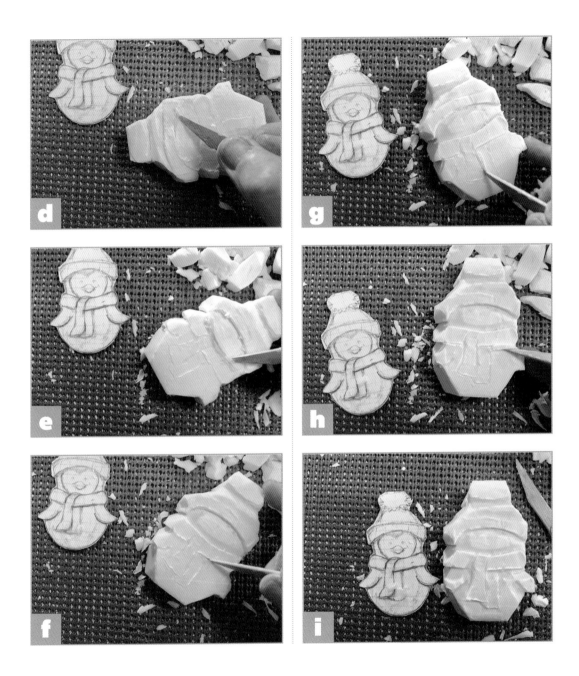

8. Carve the edge lines of the stocking cap into the sides of the soap.

9. Check the backside of the soap to be sure everything lines up and has balance.

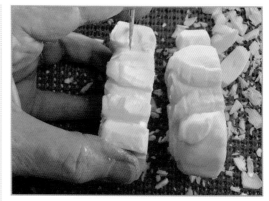

10. Trim the stocking cap tassel back so it looks more centered atop the penguin's head.

11. Shape the tassel by rounding off any square edges from the rough-out cuts.

12. Periodically, stop to review your carving. Here you see there are still a lot of square edges, so more finessing is needed. It's best to start from the top and work down.

13. I hold my carving with great care, especially while working on delicate parts. Good tool control is very important. You can see that I'm using the "push-thumb" technique on the penguin's wing. This part of the carving is delicate because there is undercutting under the wing which takes away some of the foundation the wing stands on.

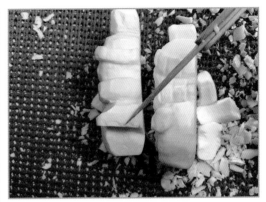

14. Cut the wing sides back.

15. After smoothing and rounding your project, it's time to start detailing. I used my small gouge to texture the tassel. With the detail knife, I detailed the rim of the stocking hat and scarf lines. I smoothed his face with my knife, gently scraping the surface. I used light stop cuts to shape the beak. Sometimes, I have to redo the stop cuts to create more depth where I feel it's needed. Over the years, I have found that I like deeper cuts for more definition. Especially when you're carving face details, it's good practice to have your tools clean and sharp.

16. Smooth the soap surface with the wet-sanding technique. Let dry.

17. He needs a cool pad so he can chill out. Center the penguin on top of the second bar and outline around the bottom. Then make a stop cut along the outline and use your chisel to chisel out soap to make a hole for him to fit snugly in. See page 77 for more tips on using mortise and tenon to make projects that stand on bases.

The best part of carving snowmen is that you can accessorize their attire with earmuffs, stocking caps, scarfs, short or long coats—there's a lot of wintry options. So decide what you want him to wear so you can carve in the details. If you want to display him on a shelf or windowsill, you can paint him up with some cheerful seasonal colors. You can carve him a snowman buddy or even a snowy family! I use my woodcarving tools for this project (see page 91), but wooden tools work fine, too.

WHAT YOU'LL NEED

- 1 Ivory bar
- template and go-by (see page 142)
- marking tool of choice
- stickpin
- detail knife
- clay-sculpting tool (optional)
- V-tool
- soap slurry

1. Prep your soap bar, center the template, and outline. Then, using a stickpin to poke a series of needle holes, mark out the interior lines of the pattern.

3. Start roughing out, using the go-by to help you keep track of areas that need to be carved away.

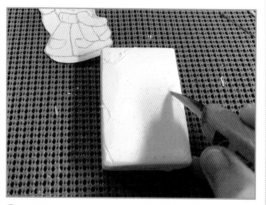

2. Make stop cuts over all of the dotted lines. Carve away all of the soap from outside the outline.

4. Optional: Use a clay-sculpting tool (see page 92) to round and smooth edges. This tool also works great for adding details to the scarf and hat.

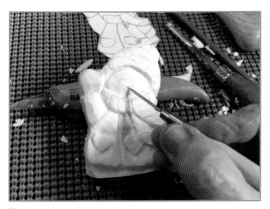

5. Etch in the carrot nose.

6. With lumpy soap slurry you can add texture to the hat tassel and rim. I also made little holes for the eyes. Next you can choose how you want to finish him—lacquer, paint, or leave him pure as the driven snow!

CARVING THE
ADVANCED PROJECTS

BEYOND IVORY: MELT-AND-POUR

While the use of Ivory bars as medium continues in Part 3, many of the projects are carved from melt-and-pour (M & P) soap. You can find melt-and-pour soap online or at specialty soap stores, or—if you're up for some home crafting—you can make it yourself (see page 111).

This kind of soap allows me to carve very thin slices for flower petals and leaves and the crisp angles needed for chip-carved designs. And for the Mother Seal with Pup Project (see page 123), melt-and-pour makes it easy to carve away large portions of soap at a time without the chipout and crumbling that would happen using other soaps.

That's why I encourage even seasoned woodcarvers who find themselves struggling with their technique to go back to the basics with soap—it's a great way to practice undercutting and carving fine details such as, for instance, the serrated edges on leaves. And while we're getting more complicated with our medium, we should also graduate to more advanced tools.

TIME FOR A TOOL UPGRADE

When it comes to doing the advanced projects that are best carved with melt-and-pour soap, you'll be happiest using traditional metal carving tools. Having the right tools is important. However, it can be a bit overwhelming to know which tool you need for which job when you go shopping for tools, whether online or at your local woodworking store. I break it down for you here so that you can choose what you need.

Knives

As with the projects in Part 2 of this book, I use the **detail knife** more than any other. Its tapered, fine point makes narrow cuts for detailing, and the blade can remove large stock when needed. It also works well for chip carving.

The **roughing knife** is a straight blade for heavier stock removal with a rounded, durable point.

Short-bladed **chip carving knives** are traditionally used to make triangular shaped cuts to create intricate designs in soap or wood.

Skews are great for cleaning out tight corners, making stop cuts, and chip carving.

V-tools

It's useful to have one small V-tool, i.e. 1/16"– 1/8", (0.16–0.3 cm), and one larger one, 1/4" (0.635 cm) for example, because they're great for carving hair or fur and texturing. The basic texturing cut is an elongated S, which gives the effect of the flow of a beard on a man or fur on an animal.

V-tools can be used for undercutting detail in relief carving. Just keep one side flat against the background.

A narrow V-tool is great for cleaning angles of all sizes.

The V-tool can be used for "sketching" or as a marking tool to outline patterns or designs. Some carvers like to use a V-tool instead of a knife for stop cuts. Always review what size V-tool will be an appropriate size for your carving piece.

Gouges

Gouges range in curvature, or "sweep," from almost flat to the shape of a U. Most tool manufacturers have a numbering system to make it easier for the carver to identify the sweep.

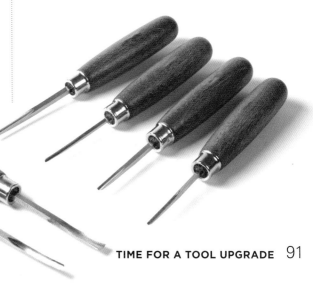

MY TIPS FOR CARVING SOAP WITH METAL TOOLS

Wear a glove. I always wear my Kevlar carving glove to protect my non-carving hand from sharp edges; the strong synthetic fiber is lightweight, flexible, and comfortable. You can purchase a lightweight Kevlar glove at your local sporting goods store, from the fishing department.

Use warm water. As with the wooden tools, keep your knives, chisels, and gouges hot and wet as you carve. I always keep a crockpot full of warm water handy to dip tools in. It's a quick and easy way to clean and warm your tools at the same time to make them better carve through soap.

Additional Tools

Clay-sculpting tools are useful for adding details and smoothing and rounding edges.

Leather stamping tools, with their unique profiles, give you exciting options for texturing and embellishing your soap projects.

Strop. Soap won't dull your tools like wood. However, soap does build up, so you will need to clean your tools periodically. I keep a damp towel nearby to wipe off my carving tools. When you do need to sharpen, use a leather strop.

I confess, bears are my weakness, especially those that are soft, furry, adorable, and friendly. Bears add rustic charm and cheer to any cabin nestled in the mountains (or any home in the city, for that matter).

This project shows you how to carve the levels needed to differentiate his nose, mouth, and ears. Once the details are done, you can learn how to texture his fur.

WHAT YOU'LL NEED

- 1 Ivory bar plus 1 bar for each tree
- template and go-by (see page 142)
- marking tool of choice
- stickpin or toothpick
- detail knife
- small gouge
- medium gouge
- small V-tool
- clay-sculpting tool
- 2 brushes, water

1. Prep your soap bar, center the template, and transfer it with your marking tool of choice.

4. Use a medium size gouge (#5 sweep) to make a stop cut around the tops of the ears.

2. Looks like the "stickpin technique" worked!

5. With the details all in, we're ready to start roughing him out.

3. Follow the dots, making stop cuts to outline the design.

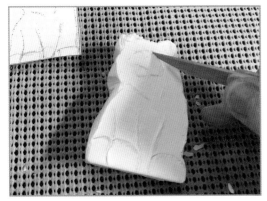

6. After removing the soap from around the bear's body, start detailing his face. First make a gentle stop cut across the nose. Then carve with the gouge face down toward the stop cut so the face is lower than the nose.

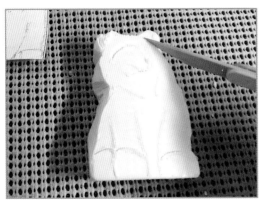

7. Make a stop cut on top of the head to give definition between head and ears. The ears will be set back so the forehead will be higher than ears. The forehead will be lower than the nose level.

8. Start shaping the legs and feet. I used a #3 gouge to round and smooth.

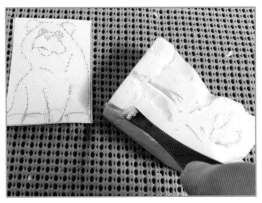

9. Use a small gouge to dig the soap out between the legs and feet.

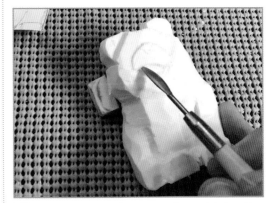

10. Use a clay-sculpting tool to add details and smooth and round edges.

11. Use only gentle pressure when adding in the nose.

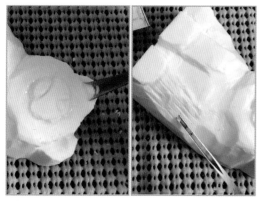

12. Start shaping and cleaning the ears with a medium size gouge (#5). Continue detailing him by using a small V-tool to make fur lines. He is a real cutie patootie!

Trees

13. Add a few trees and you have a "beary" rustic theme for your kitchen, bath, or mudroom.

With these kritters you can personalize your kitchen, naturally, or even a mudroom with a farm theme. I personally like roosters and hens, so they make up a big part of my kitchen décor. After I'd made a hen and then a cow (since there's a lot of cow lovers out there), I figured I had to complete the barnyard theme, so this little piggy . . . stayed home. All you need is an Ivory bar for each kritter and the usual set of tools, plus the templates and go-bys (see page 143). Now let's carve some cute little kitchen kritters!

 Cow

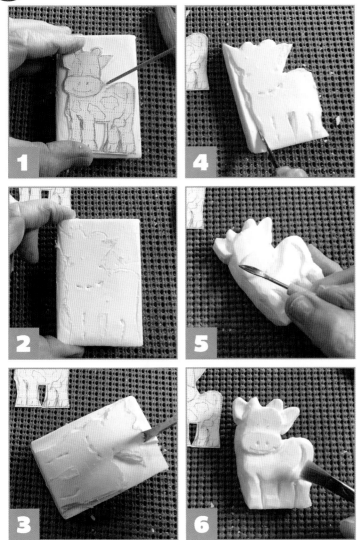

1. Prep your soap bar, center the template, and outline.

2. It's best to add details such as hooves, legs, face, ears, and horns with a toothpick since it can get into tiny areas.

3. Using your detail knife and your #3 gouge, make stop cuts over the outlines you marked out earlier.

4. Carve around the project until all soap is removed from the outside of pattern. Now it's time to add the details for the legs and hooves.

5. Adding details takes time, but it's a lot of fun. Lower the cow's face down so the nose becomes the highest point on the head. Carving under the chin will drop the level of the body, giving some separation from body to head.

6. Dry brush any tiny chips, then wet sand to help wash any uneven edges until they're smooth and round.

Pig

Okay, now let's do this cute, plump little pig with a great personality and smile . . .

1. Prep your soap, center your template, and outline (I used a toothpick). If it's helpful, you can poke a stickpin through the template to outline internal pattern lines. Or you can just sketch details in with a toothpick after lifting the template off.

2. Using your detail knife, carve over your lines to make stop cuts.

3. Carve around the project until all soap is removed from outside the outline.

4. Start adding details. Make a stop cut on top of the head and carve toward the head. This will drop the level so the ears will be lower. Since my #3 gouge has the same profile as the top of the nose, I used it instead of my knife to make my stop cut. Carve face level down so the cheek on the piggy is at a higher level. Then carve in the snout.

5. Keep working your way down the body until everything is roughed out.

6. Use a clay-sculpting tool to round off the edges. Dry brush, wet sand, and you're finished!

Hen

Roosters and hens are always popular. Let's carve a hen resting on her straw bed . . .

1. Prep your soap, center your template, and outline with a toothpick. You can either sketch in all the interior detail lines or use the stickpin technique to outline.

2. Stop cut over the outline with a detail knife or your gouge of choice (I used my trusty #3). Stop cut, then gouge toward the stop cut. Layer down little by little until all soap has been removed. Leave a little extra soap around the beak so you have plenty of soap to work with, just in case the soap is brittle.

3. Use your go-by for the details.

4. Use a small gouge to add feathers.

5. For the straw bed, use a small V-tool. Dry brush, wet sand, and let it dry. Finish as you like!

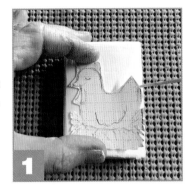

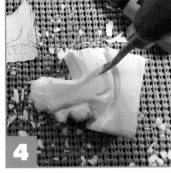

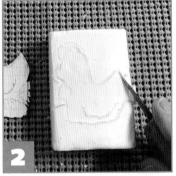

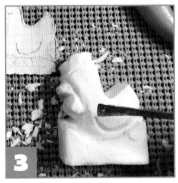

PAMPERED PUP

With her personalized puppy pillow and doggie treat, this little pup certainly is pampered! Have fun painting this cutie with spots or just one of your favorite colors. Then personalize the pillow with paw prints, flowers, or colors that coordinate with the room she will be displayed in. Want to add more detail? Add a favorite doggie toy!

WHAT YOU'LL NEED

- 2 Ivory bars
- template and go-by (see page 144)
- detail knife
- skew knife
- stickpin
- marking tool of choice
- large gouge
- small gouge

1. Well, you know the drill by now . . . prep your soap and so on . . .

2. Notice I have my pattern sitting up higher on the bar—that extra soap on the bottom is for the tenon. Later this tenon will fit into the mortise in the pup's bed. At this stage you can sketch the details of the face and legs, or you can draw the pattern onto tracing paper and mark the outline with the stickpin technique.

3. Remove the unwanted soap from around the pup—stop cut, then cut with knife or gouge, removing soap layer by layer.

4. With a small gouge that matches the profile of the pup's mouth, make a stop cut, applying very little pressure so the soap doesn't crack and crumble.

5. Use a detail knife to make stop cuts for the collar and under the chin. As with the mouth, the soap for the nose will be very fragile. Make a gentle stop cut, then scrape away soap under this stop cut. The nose will be your highest point on this carving.

7. Now let's make her bed. Make a mortise on a second bar of soap by boring out soap with a chisel (see page 77). On the bottom of the puppy's feet, outline a tenon to fit into the mortise. Be sure to position her in the center of the second bar.

6. Continue adding details. Use the skew knife to do gentle scraping and shaping. Every so often I sit back to look at my work to see if more areas need deeper cuts for contrast reasons. Once all the roughing out is done and the details are in, add eyes—a toothpick does the job.

8. I think I'll call her . . . "Cuddles." I embellished her pillow bed with her name and gave her a bone. Whether you paint her or not, be sure to coat your project with lacquer to preserve it.

CAT WITH ATTITUDE

1 HR

I haven't met a cat yet that hasn't had an attitude. "Attitude" can mean a number of things, but for this cat, it means she thinks she's a princess. Sitting prim and proper on her soft pillow with tassels, with her fancy pink collar and heart-shaped charm, she is spoiled to the hilt!

I chose not to apply a lot of paint on this project so the paint wouldn't draw attention away from my detail work. But you can add more charm with more paint or give her more bling by gluing a few rhinestones to her collar. While this cat would probably enjoy bath time, she would enjoy more being displayed on a shelf, table, or windowsill where she can be admired.

WHAT YOU'LL NEED

- 2 Ivory bars
- template and go-by (see page 144)
- detail knife
- marking tool of choice
- small gouge (#3)
- large gouge
- 2 brushes, water

1. Prep your soap bar, center the template, and outline the template.

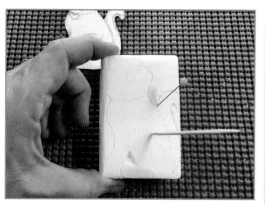

2. Add lines marking her legs, back, and facial features.

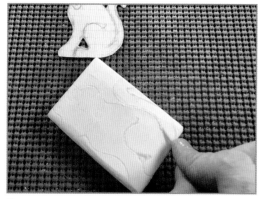

3. Using the detail knife, go over the markings and make stop cuts.

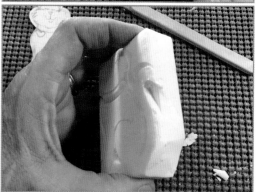

4. Begin roughing out. You can use your detail knife and, for curved areas, a gouge. I always start up at the top and work my way down. Carve under the chin and add the legs, tail, and the outer lines of the cat.

5. I used a number of different tools on this project, including a small gouge for making the stop cut around the ears.

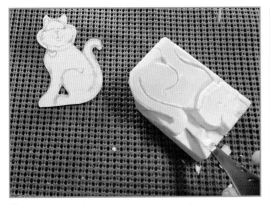

6. Keep working away at removing unwanted soap. Leave a little extra soap near the ears and the tail since these areas are fragile and can easily break.

7. Clean your work area and prepare for detailing mode.

Detailing

8. I have found it best practice to carve the face first. Say you carve the whole body and then do the face, and then you find you aren't happy with the results of the face. Then you may have to re-carve the whole project, since the face is the focal point of a carving.

9. Make a gentle stop cut with a #3 gouge on top of the cat's head. Use a knife or #3 gouge to make a level for the ears so that the ears will be set back from the forehead.

10. Make the same stop cut for the cheeks. Use the #3 gouge to plane down the face so that the nose is the highest point of the face.

11. Use the detail knife to add more detail to the eyes, nose, and mouth.

12. Shape and clean your kitty's ears.

13. Keep turning your project around. It makes it easier to carve, plus it lets you see areas you've missed carving or need to clean.

Finishing

14. Dry brush and wet sand. Paint your cat if you wish. Remember to seal your project with spray lacquer so the paint will glide well on the soap surface (see page 38).

The Pillow

15. My cool cat with attitude is ready for bedtime . . .

16. She needs a pillow—so let's carve a fancy pillow with tassels.

17. Prep your soap, place your template over one end, and outline with a toothpick.

18. Start carving the slope down all four edges of the pillow.

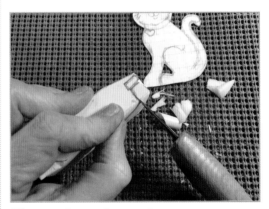

19. Rough out the tassels.

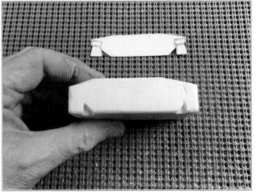

20. Now let's detail the pillow.

21. Use your small gouge to create the roundness of the top part of the tassel. Holding your tool upside down gives you a round-over effect, so you can make a small ball-like top of the tassel. Carve all four tassels this way.

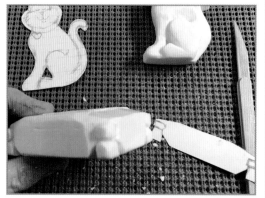

22. All the roughing out is finished. Now we need to do some finessing.

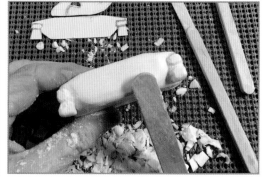

23. Use your large gouge to smooth and round the edges.

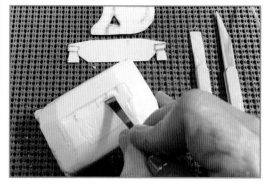

24. Next mortise out an area so the cat has an area to rest on the pillow. Set the cat vertically in the center of the bar. I mortised down about ¼"–½" (0.5–1 cm), just enough so that the cat is cradled in the pillow.

25. Dry brush, wet sand, and let dry. It's up to you whether to paint her or not. Either way, lacquer for a lasting finish.

WORKSHOP: MELT-AND-POUR SOAP

To make melt-and-pour soap, all you need is a coconut-rich soap base and some common kitchen equipment. It's easy, quick, and affordable. Fun, too!

This activity involves melting a soap base that you buy online or from a hobby or specialty store, then adding your own choices of fragrances and colors. I use a coconut-rich base that makes smooth, creamy, and solid soap—perfect for intricate carving projects.

WHAT YOU'LL NEED

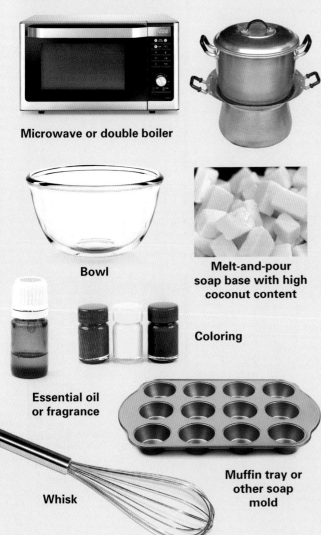

Microwave or double boiler

Bowl

Melt-and-pour soap base with high coconut content

Essential oil or fragrance

Coloring

Whisk

Muffin tray or other soap mold

1. First, melt the soap base. You can use either a double boiler or a microwave—just be sure to follow the instructions on the package. When it's melted, you can add fragrance and/or color. I use combinations of the three primary colors (yellow, red, and blue) to make every color in the rainbow and then some. Since the base is white and creamy, the resulting soap tends to look more pastel. Use a whisk to mix in your fragrance and/or color(s).

2. Mold. Once you have the color consistency you desire, pour the melted soap base into a mold. You can buy specialty molds or you can use an old muffin pan or other mold that will shape the soap into a bar or cake.

3. Cool and carve. After the soap cools and hardens fully (I allow 12 hours at room temperature), remove the bars from their molds, and you are ready to carve. Another nice thing about melt-and-pour is that there is no prepping of the soap bar—it's logo-free.

SPRING BUTTERFLIES

15 MIN

As holidays go with the seasons, so do the decorations in my house. With Easter and spring fast approaching one year, I wanted to carve something other than bunnies and Easter eggs. Now, don't get me wrong, they do make adorable projects for the soap dish, but I wanted to carve something different. Spring produces flowers, bumblebees, and butterflies, and I figured butterflies would be better received than bumblebees, so butterflies and flowers it shall be. See page 5 for what I mean . . .

This project will guide you through carving a medium-to-high relief. Then you will uplift the butterflies' wings so they appear to be taking flight.

WHAT YOU'LL NEED

- 1 melt-and-pour soap bar
- template and go-by (see page 144)
- stickpin
- small gouge
- detail knife

1. Transfer the pattern using the stickpin technique. Make deep stop cuts along the outline and all interior pattern lines.

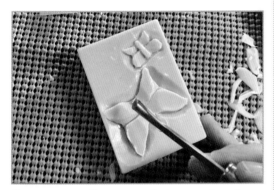

2. Use a small gouge to help round and smooth both butterflies' bodies.

3. Undercut one of the bigger butterfly's wings and gently pull upward on the soap. The wingtip should rise from the background into high relief.

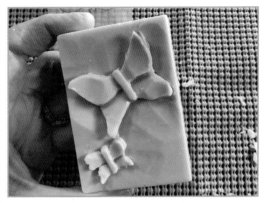

4. This view shows the lift under the butterfly's wing.

5. You can make butterflies from all kinds of colors. If you cut a bar of soap in half, you can make two for the price of one!

> **TIP: Undercutting**, or carving away soap from under the edge of a flower petal, say, or butterfly wing in a relief, adds shadow and drama. Be careful, though: undercut soap is fragile!

ROSE RELIEF

2 HRS

This tutorial covers all three major techniques used in relief style carving: undercutting, layering, and detailing. The characteristics of melt-and-pour soap combined with the technique involved will accelerate your soap carving education. Notice the serrated edges of the petals and how well the soap holds detail. A bar of soap like this will certainly add beauty and elegance to any shower, bath, or sink.

WHAT YOU'LL NEED

- 1 melt-and-pour soap bar
- template and go-by (see page 145)
- stickpin
- gouge or clay-sculpting tool (optional)
- detail knife

1. To transfer the pattern onto your bar of soap, use transfer paper, and with a stickpin poke a series of dots running along the lines of the design. Make sure you have good lighting

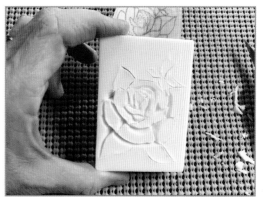

3. Keep your go-by near to keep track of which side of your stop to cut at a 45-degree angle. Deep angles make shadows, which is what you want—more depth.

4. Keep working your way around the rose, rounding over.

2. Make stop cuts over your dotted lines. I tried to make my stop cuts as deep as I could. Keep your knife sharp, clean, and hot.

5. You can use a gouge or a clay-sculpting tool to give the petals more depth and movement.

6. Undercut the leaves and petals—it adds so much realism.

7. With your detail knife, gently swoop down to the center of the leaf and then sweep back up to the outer edge. This technique can change flat leaves to leaves with movement.

8. I added serrations to the leaves for a final touch of realism. Carving with my blade oriented toward the middle of the bar gives me better control of my detail knife.

HUMMINGBIRD KEEPSAKE BOX

While I chose to do a low relief, this design can just as easily be carved as a medium or high relief—the more pronounced the cuts, the more dimension and depth you add to the project. This project will sharpen your awareness of detail, especially when carving the hummingbird's feathers. Embellishing a keepsake box will add even more meaning to those special mementos inside.

WHAT YOU'LL NEED

- 2 melt-and-pour soap bars
- template (see page 146)
- detail knife
- long detail knife
- gouge
- ruler
- 2 brushes, water
- chisel

1. Place just a little bit of tape on each side to help keep the pattern in place.

2. Holding your knife over the top like a pencil, outline right through the template.

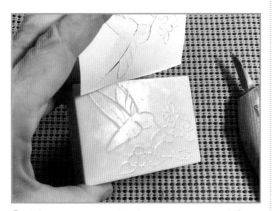

3. If you want to check your progress, lift one side of the template and take a peek.

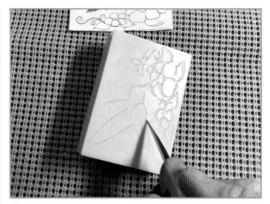

4. With a detail knife, deepen your stop cuts. Make sure you keep your knife sharp, clean, and hot.

5. Make your rough-out cuts. As always, have your go-by near for reference.

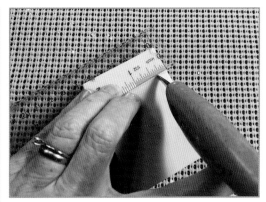

6. Use your long detail knife to do some undercutting. Slice right under the wing of the hummingbird to give it lift, just like the butterfly project. Save the beak for last since there is a risk of it fracturing or breaking off while carving.

8. For the bottom half of the keepsake box, measure out walls ¼" (0.5 cm) thick. Make stop cuts for all four walls.

7. To give the leaves more interest, sculpt them inward with a sweeping motion and add serrated edges. Then wet sand.

9. Use a gouge to excavate soap. Then, to scrape the bottom and straighten the interior walls, switch to a chisel. To finish, wet sand and let it dry. Now it's ready to store treasures.

RADIANT CROSS

The chip-carved medallions (see page 129) inspired me to make more chip-carved projects. My next was a cross. I copied one of my favorite patterns from Marty Leenhouts's website, *www.mychipcarving.com* (reproduced in this book with his permission) and sized it down to fit my bar of soap. I noticed as soon as I laid my pattern on the soap the moisture from the melt-and-pour soap adhered to the pattern—what a great find! The tackiness of the soap helps the pattern stay in place while carving. I display my cross year round to remind me of all my blessings.

I hold my knife at a 65-degree angle so I can get great depth and dimension with the soap.

WHAT YOU'LL NEED

- 1 melt-and-pour soap bar, 1" x 3½" x 5" (2.5 x 9 x 12 cm)
- template (see page 146)
- detail knife
- toothpick

1. I outlined with my detail knife, right through the paper. My detail knife has a longer blade and more tapered tip compared to my chip carving knife, so I prefer it for this project.

2. Good lighting is important. So is a clean, hot knife, so have a cup of hot water nearby.

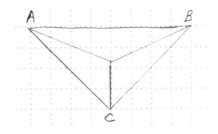

3. Holding your knife at 65 degrees, make the first rough-out cut, toward yourself. From point A to point B, the knife is plunged into the soap. Gently pull your knife out. Turn your soap so you can comfortably make the next cut. Repeat the first step, but this time cut from B to C.

4. The last cut is from C to A. I have found slicing and lifting works well. Be sure your knife is sharp, clean, and hot.

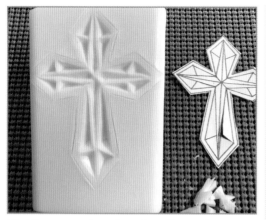

5. There may be a few tiny slivers that are hard to clear away, which is normal. Use a toothpick to help clear any slivers and flakes. I burnished the soap to help accentuate the angles.

6. To embellish the ground level of the project, I needed to make a stop cut completely around the cross. I wanted my ground level to be about ¼" (0.5 cm) deeper than the top surface of my cross. When making a stop cut, be sure your knife is straight up and down.

7. Shave the soap surrounding the cross, bringing the level down ⅛" (0.3 cm). Then go back to do some texturing. Hold your detail knife very flat and move your wrist up and down in a waving motion. The neat thing with chip carving is that you can have just one pattern and make several designs from it just by changing the positive and negative spaces.

2 HRS

I wanted to try out all styles of carving in this book, especially carving in the round. But I wanted to do something different than the usual turtle or a leaping dolphin. So the idea came to carve a mother seal, also called a "cow," showing love, compassion, and protection to her young pup. In order to show this, I had to carve one of her flippers draped over the back of the pup. I decided to paint only the noses and eyes so the viewer can see the facets and details from the carving tools—I was going for a stylized appearance. And to give my project more dimension, I added a second block of soap to make a higher base.

WHAT YOU'LL NEED

- 1 melt-and-pour soap bar, 3" x 4" x 5" (8 x 10 x 13 cm)
- a 2nd bar of the same size for additional base (optional)
- template and go-by (see page 146)
- detail knife
- gouge (optional)

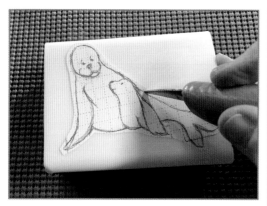

use a gouge. Deepen your stop cuts and carve layer by layer. Remember, when you have a lot of soap to remove, it's essential to have a cup of hot water to keep your knife clean and hot.

1. Center the template high on the bar. Seal, pup, and platform are all carved from one piece. Outline the pattern with your detail knife. Cut the interior lines with the knife as well, right through the paper. Your stop cuts should be deep.

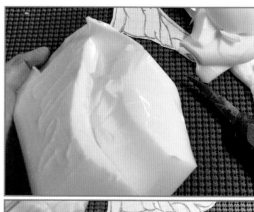

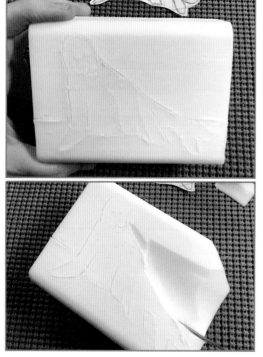

2. With the pattern lines transferred through deep stop cuts, it's time to rough out. I used detail knives, but you can also

3. Carving in the round means you need to keep moving your piece around to maintain a balanced look. Are we having fun yet? YES!

4. Cut in to form the base. Keep your go-by near for reference.

5. Pay special attention to how the mother seal has her flipper around the back of her young pup. Her flipper will be the point closest to the viewer's eye. Mother's head level will be behind the pup. A long knife gives you flexibility with the blade, whereas a shorter knife is more rigid to work with. I carved the mother seal's neck and chin all in one sweeping motion going upward. I did the same sweeping motion on top of both the mother seal's and pup's noses. In the end you'll have something really special!

30 MIN

Snowflakes are simple and fun and look great displayed in a soap dish. They add a nice touch near a sink or bath during the winter months. To create a festive holiday theme, you can add a snowman or Santa to your snowflakes.

WHAT YOU'LL NEED

- 1 Ivory bar for each snowflake
- templates (see page 145)
- toothpick
- detail knife
- gouge
- ruler (optional)
- 2 brushes, water

1. Prep your soap bar(s). Instead of placing your template in the middle, place it at one end. This way there will be less waste. Outline.

2. Remove the template and outline the pattern to more depth using a toothpick—it's difficult for a detail knife to get into such small areas.

3. I cut off the excess soap because it's easier to work with a smaller area.

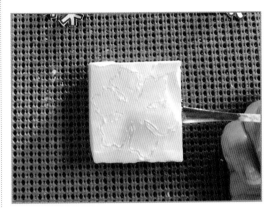

4. Use a gouge (#5) to make a stop cut for the outer edges of snowflake.

5. To establish a consistent ground level measure and make a line. All your stop cuts will go down to this level.

6. Use your detail knife to make stop cuts on the straight lines of the snowflake. Once you have all the stop cuts made, you can cut in from the sides toward your stop cuts. This develops the ground level.

8. Using a toothpick, clean out any excess chips from the gaps in the snowflake. Also dry brush the surfaces clean.

7. Continue carving with your detail knife and reestablish the curved ends with your gouge as necessary. Cut and smooth edges at the same time.

9. Finally, wet sand to smooth the soap. It's complete! If you want to keep carving, cut down all the way to make it a carving in the round.

I'm super excited to share my chip-carved medallion project because chip carving is not something you normally see in soap carving. Once I found out about melt-and-pour soap, I realized that it's a lot like carving wood. Chip carving is all about angles and how you hold your knife. All you need is square melt-and-pour soap bars cut in half, templates (draw your own, or check for patterns online), and a detail knife. In addition, together they make an artistically interesting decoration set piece that can be displayed in any bathroom or kitchen sink.

30 MIN Medallions

1a

After outlining the template, make stop cuts along the lines.

1b

Chip away at the soap. Continue to carve to add definition. Dry brush and wet sand.

2a

After transferring the template and making stop cuts, rough out the soap around the outline of the star.

2b

For a carving in the round, continue your cuts all the way through.

3a

Transfer the template and make stop cuts along the lines.

3b

Chip out the radial pattern. Dry brush and wet sand as needed.

Soap flowers for sale in Chiang Rai, Thailand

BROADER HORIZONS: SIAM (THAI) SOAP FLOWER CARVING

Several years ago, I discovered Siam (Thai) soap flower carving online, and I was absolutely amazed at how the carvers could make such elaborate flowers out of soap. With the use of just one long detail knife, they create thin, delicate petals, and then, using the same knife, they push the petals upward or downward to make the flowers look super realistic.

The more I watched this beautiful form of soap carving, the more I wanted to learn. I decided to teach myself. First, I tried carving the flowers out of Ivory, Dial, and Dove, but the flowers just didn't look the same as what I was seeing online; these soaps' textures would not allow me to carve very thin petals or move the petals with the knife. I needed a soap that was more soft and pliable.

My search led me to a soap company near me. I showed all three store representatives my favorite tutorials so they could help me. They were amazed: they'd never seen soap carving like this before. At once, all three suggested

"M & P" soap. They explained to me that melt-and-pour (M & P) soap has more oil content than over-the-counter soap bars. I bought five pounds, went home, and started carving flowers. It worked perfectly!

At first carving the flowers was challenging, but the more I practiced the easier it became. I used my long, thin detail knife, dipping it often in warm water, to carve flower petals with ease. The water acts as a lubricant and the heat makes the soap more flexible.

The next day, I went back to let my new friends at the soap company know that their recommendations had been perfect. Fifteen-plus pounds of soap later, and I've carved many beautiful flowers. Finding M & P has opened new doors for me as a soap carver. Furthermore, the relationship with the soap company that began with me bringing in my Siam soap flower tutorials continues, and has led to them putting my carvings on display for other customers to see what you can do with soap.

THE SOAP FLOWER'S ORIGINS

Thailand's art of soap carving grew out its more established tradition of fruit and vegetable carving, known as *kae sa luk* and which is as old as Thai culture itself.

In the northern city of Sukhothai ("Dawn of Happiness") in the 1300s, when it was the capital of the first Kingdom of Siam, the king expected his meals to not only be delicious but also beautiful—dazzling, even—to look at. His royal chefs responded by carving fruits and vegetables, including watermelons, onions, and carrots, into majestic natural forms, like those of the orchid, the chrysanthemum, and the lotus. The tradition flourished through 600 years of Thai monarchy.

But after the 1932 Siamese Revolution and the ensuing decades of military rule, the art of *kae sa luk* declined. Only in recent years has it been rediscovered and taught again in schools and cultural centers.

While fruit and vegetable carvings are meant to be admired for a short time and then eaten, some carvers in modern Thailand, especially in the street markets of the northern tourist cities, use soap as a medium to make longer-lasting replications of *kae sa luk*.

THAI SOAP FLOWER

1 HR

My first impression of these beautiful soap flowers was a little overwhelming. My question was, how to carve them? But once you know how they are created, you'll overcome that first impression and come to make them with ease. Each one is unique and lovely. You will enjoy making these and even more enjoy giving them as gifts!

WHAT YOU'LL NEED

- 1 melt-and-pour soap bar
- melon ball tool or small cardboard circle template
- detail knife
- hot water and towel

1. First, center your melon ball tool in the middle of the soap bar. Press the tool down to make an impression on the soap. If you don't have this tool, you can make a circle out of cardstock and use a detail knife to outline.

2. Use a stickpin to poke little holes indicating where the first petals will be.

3. Make a deep stop cut over the circle outline.

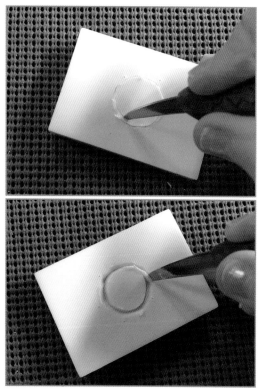

4. Holding your knife at a 45-degree angle, rough out, cutting with your blade toward the stop cut. Cut and lift out and away from the circle.

5. Re-mark your petals if necessary.

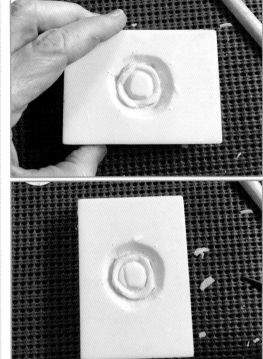

6. Make a deep stop cut to develop the first petal from point to point. For your second cut, hold your knife at a 45-degree angle and cut toward the stop cut, lifting the soap as you cut.

7. Repeat the above steps four more times to complete the first ring of petals. Round off any squareness from the center. The next row will be four petals. Each petal is placed between two petals of the first row. This staggers the petals to add fullness, separation, and definition to the flower.

8. Make your rows working outward from the center of the flower. Once the center petals are made, you can start on the outer rows.

9. The next row of five petals is staggered as well. Keep making rows until you reach the size of flower you want.

10. Add leaves, ribbons, or lace to give your project balance. Who would have guessed that in this bar of soap there was a beautiful flower hiding all along?

TEMPLATES AND GO-BYS

Copy at 125%.

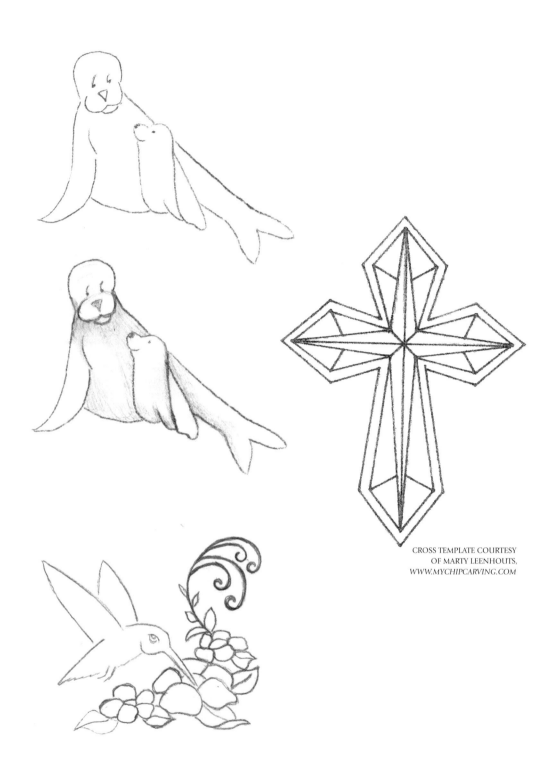

CROSS TEMPLATE COURTESY
OF MARTY LEENHOUTS,
WWW.MYCHIPCARVING.COM

INDEX

Page numbers in *italics* indicate projects/templates.